CW00822675

THE PRAYER OF THE KABBALIST

© 2007 Kabbalah Centre International, Inc.

All rights reserved. No part of this publication may be
reproduced or transmitted in any form or by any means,
electronic or mechanical, including photocopying,
recording, or by any information storage and retrieval
system, without permission in writing from the publisher,
except by a reviewer who wishes to quote brief passages
in connection with a review written for inclusion in a
magazine, newspaper, or broadcast.

Kabbalah Publishing is a registered DBA of
Kabbalah Centre International, Inc.

For further information:

The Kabbalah Centre
155 E. 48th St., New York, NY 10017
1062 S. Robertson Blvd., Los Angeles, CA 90035

1.800.Kabbalah
www.kabbalah.com

First Edition August 2007
Second Printing November 2007
Printed in Canada
ISBN10: 1-57189-575-2
ISBN13: 978-1-57189-575-2

Design: HL Design (Hyun Min Lee) www.hldesignco.com

1 2 **THE** 3 4 5 6 7 8
9 10 11 12 **PRAYER**
OF 13 14 15 16 17 18
19 20 21 **THE** 22 23
24 **KABBALIST** 25
26 27 28 29 30 31 32
33 34 35 36 37 38 39
40 41 (42)

THE 42 - LETTER NAME OF GOD

YEHUDA BERG

www.kabbalah.com™

ACKNOWLEDGMENTS

To the people who make my life better each and every day—my parents, the Rav and Karen, my brother Michael, my wife Michal and our children—and to those who are such an important part of revealing this wisdom through their gifts and support: Billy Phillips, Stephanie Schottel, Peter Guzzardi, Hyun Min Lee, and Phyllis Henrici. Thank you all.

TABLE OF CONTENTS

The forty-two lettered Name is entrusted only to him who is virtuous, meek, middle-aged, free from bad temper, sober, and not insistent on his rights. And he who knows it, is heedful thereof, and observes it in purity, is beloved above and popular below, feared by man, and inherits two worlds, this world and the future world.

—The Talmud

CHAPTER ONE
THE ANSWER

If you go to *Google*, the Internet search engine, and type in the following question *exactly* as it appears below:

What is the answer to life, the universe, and everything?

Google delivers the following answer:

The answer to life, the universe, and everything = 42

If you don't believe me, give it a try yourself. Google will tell you that the answer to life, the universe, and everything equals 42. And here's the reason why.

In Douglas Adams's best-selling book, *The Hitchhiker's Guide to the Galaxy*, a highly advanced supercomputer nicknamed Deep Thought is programmed to ponder such questions. When asked for the answer to life, the universe, and everything, the computer begins its complex computations and continues calculating for seven and a half million years. Finally, Deep Thought produces an answer:

"Forty-two," said Deep Thought, with infinite majesty
and calm.

Forty-two might seem to be a peculiar response given the circumstances, but it is definitely not the first time that this number has made an appearance in history.

* * *

An Old Testament story tells of the Israelites wandering the desert for 40 years. The biblical text, which—according to the great sages—never wastes a single letter, goes to the trouble of mentioning how the Israelites were forced to camp out in 42 different locations. The great kabbalists asked the question: Why 42? Why not 41 or 43?

* * *

In the New Testament, Matthew 1:17 (King James Version), the following text appears:

"So all the generations from Abraham to David are fourteen generations; and from David until the carrying away into Babylon are fourteen generations; and from carrying away into Babylon unto Christ are fourteen generations."

Christians scholars have long pondered the mystical significance of the number of generations referred to in this passage—three fourteens, which total 42!

* * *

The prophet Muhammad had 42 transcribers record the revelations that he received from the angel Gabriel to form the Quran.

* * *

4

When the sun's rays travel 91 million miles to brighten our planet after rain showers, we often see a rainbow. Sunbeams must reflect off water molecules at precisely a 42-degree angle in order to produce this beautiful, multi-colored arc.

* * *

Scribes have carefully copied the biblical scroll of the Old Testament in the same precise manner for some 3,400 years. The writing on the parchment is broken into columns, each of which has 42 lines of scripture.

* * *

The holy city of Jerusalem, sacred to Christians, Jews and Muslims, covers an area of 42 square miles.

IT'S NO MYSTERY

As you can see, 42 is an intriguing and significant number. Kabbalah has an interesting, and very specific, understanding of the reasons why and, more importantly, just how we can harness the power of this number to transform our lives.

Throughout history, our most challenging questions about life, death, good, and evil were answered with the same old response:

God works in mysterious ways.

The kabbalists laughed and cried over that answer. Why? They laughed at the ignorance and foolishness of it. They cried because it's just not true, and it's a human tragedy that people have been fed this inaccurate, cryptic answer for centuries. So let's understand this from the get-go: God does not work in mysterious ways, at least not according to Kabbalah. God works in simple ways; therefore, the answers to life's questions are really quite simple. The reason we never found authentic, satisfying answers from religion is this: the religious establishment, for some 2,000 years, did everything in its power to keep Kabbalah from people like you and me.

But that time is behind us. Today the technology of Kabbalah and all of the answers contained therein are ours for the taking. The answers belong to each and every one of us, and we know this thanks to a sacred, world-altering text that came into existence a very long time ago.

THE ORIGINAL *HITCHHIKER'S GUIDE*

You could say that a kabbalist named Rav Shimon bar Yochai wrote the original *Hitchhiker's Guide to the Galaxy* some 2,000 years ago. In fact, not only did this great kabbalist provide a road map of our galaxy, he explained the entire cosmos, including the universe we experience through our five senses, as well as the reality that exists just beyond the radar of human perception. What he really wrote was a deeply revealing guide to the human soul.

This quintessential text is called the *Zohar*, which means the *Book of Splendor*. And from this great and mysterious book, we learn that the number 42 is, indeed, the secret answer to everything! Deep Thought, the computer in *The Hitchhiker's Guide*, had it absolutely right.

And here's why.

IT'S ALL IN THE NAME

The number 42 refers to the **42-Letter Name of God**. But let me be clear here. We are not referring to a literal name like Butch or Sundance, Lennon or McCartney, 50 Cent or Eminem. We are talking about the energy and power that a name can evoke. God doesn't really have a name like you and I do, but the force that we call God does have power—an infinite amount, to be precise.

THE KEYS TO CREATION

We have access to this power, and we activate it via a particular ignition key. This is what *name* really means; it's the key to the one and only true ignition. It's a combination of letters that gives us direct access to a specific type of divine energy that can dramatically transform our lives. Just as the shape of a key is the mechanism by which one unlocks a door or starts the engine of a car, the shape of the letters in the 42-Letter Name of God has the ability to unlock the Gates of Heaven and ignite the engines of Creation. Now, that's some powerful stuff.

These remarkable forces can awaken healing, prosperity, love, courage, and foresight. There is even an energy that can remove all those doubts swirling in your mind right now about the believability of what you have read so far. In fact, the only reason you suffer doubt is because you have not been able to unlock an energy force known as *certainty*! This particular force, this unique Name of God, has the ability to dissolve any and all doubts you have about achieving unending fulfillment, connection, and joy.

In the pages of this book, you'll learn how to unlock all of the energy contained in the 42-Letter Name of God and use it to create powerful change in your life and the lives of those around you.

Indeed, 42 really *is* the answer.

CHAPTER TWO

THE
QUESTION

QUESTIONS, QUESTIONS, AND MORE QUESTIONS

One of the characters in *The Hitchhiker's Guide to the Galaxy*, named Loonquawl, was quite astonished by Deep Thought's answer to the question of life.

> *"Forty-two!" yelled Loonquawl. "Is that all you've got to show for seven and a half million years' work?"*
>
> *"I checked it very thoroughly," said the computer, "and that quite definitely is the answer. I think the problem, to be quite honest with you, is that you've never actually known what the question is."*

Deep Thought's point is a good one. How do we know that we've asked the right question? How could we ever be sure in light of the fact that we have a bazillion questions. The questions we have about our origin, our purpose, and our ultimate destiny are endless. It would be a relief to have just one question, to be honest.

Why are there so many questions?

Questions are part of the physical world's very nature. Fortunately, questions are just one side to the coin.

REVEALING REALITY

According to Kabbalah, there are two realities. One reality we see quite clearly. This is the reality you perceive right now, at this very moment. You experience this reality every day. Look directly around you. Now look at the news you receive of the larger world. See all the chaos, the pain, the fighting, the disease, the dying, and the dread? Uncertainty and doubt also flourish here; for that reason our minds create an endless barrage of questions—unending queries into the meaning of life, the meaning of our existence, the meaning of suffering and evil, and the whereabouts of God.

Okay, that is all part of the first reality. But there is another reality, one that you cannot discern with your eyes. Nor can you touch, smell, hear, or taste it. Despite this, it is as real as the nose on your face and the atoms you learned about in grade school. This realm is simultaneously infinite yet perfectly complete. In fact, your soul used to dwell in this space, this World of Answers. At one time, you knew all of the answers.

I know. I know. You think you would remember being a divine genius, and we'll discuss that point in a moment, but for now know that these two realities can best be described as follows:

- **Reality One—The World of Questions.**

- **Reality Two—The World of Answers.**

Now that you know there are two realities, you can begin to understand the problem at the heart of human existence. Here it is: we look for answers inside a World of Questions. We look for answers right here in the physical world of chaos. Naturally it's a futile effort. *Answers* do not reside in this world. This world is only about questions. It is filled with questions. It abounds with questions. It is flooded with questions: questions about love, questions about business, questions about our existence, questions about friendship, questions about human suffering.

We believe, mistakenly, that we will find our answers right here. Not true. *Here* there are no long-term solutions or answers. Our physical world, with all of its endless information, only delivers short-term fixes and makeshift remedies. Problems recur; pain comes back; aggravation and disorder stage a repeat performance. We are left disoriented and lost and wondering:

How did I get stuck in this World of Questions? Why is the World of Answers so hard to find? Why do two realities exist? And finally:

WHY AM I HERE ASKING THESE QUESTIONS?

Because you asked the Creator to hide all of the answers—that's why.

CHAPTER THREE

A TIME
BEFORE
QUESTIONS

THE QUESTION OF CREATION

Yes, there once was a time when no questions existed. A time when your soul was never left wondering why or how or what if. A time when there was only God and all the divine wisdom that is God. As I mentioned before, our souls once dwelled in this place, this World of Answers. In this world, we wanted for nothing—not material wealth, not happiness, and certainly not answers. This is because the Creator gave us *everything* we needed. We possessed all the joy and wisdom imaginable. We had it all—except for one thing. Can you guess what was missing?

It's the same thing that's missing when you cheat on a test and make an A. It's what's missing when you win the lottery even though you never worked a day in your life. It's what would be lacking if you possessed a body like Mr. or Ms. Universe yet you had never stepped foot in a gym.

What's missing in these scenarios is the same thing that was missing in the World of Answers—the fulfillment and sense of pleasure that goes along with earning our reward and discovering the answers on our own. Having it all might make you feel lucky for a moment, but after the initial awe wears off, this state of existence starts feeling like a charitable handout.

How much fun is there in taking a handout? Let's just say it has its limits. This being the case, you asked the Creator to hide all the joy. Hide all the happiness. Conceal all the answers. You asked the Creator to place you in a different world, one at odds with the blissful reality into which you were originally born.

Why?

You did this so that you could find endless joy and fulfill-ment by virtue of your own effort.

Your own effort!

That's it. That's the reason for life. That's the reason for the entire universe. That's the reason for everything. It's the reason the atom was created. It's the reason the Big Bang took place. It's the reason the animal, vegetable, and mineral kingdoms were brought into existence. We, the souls of humanity, wanted to come into a world of darkness and chaos in order to trans-form it into a world of Light and order by way of our own indi-vidual and collective effort.

In other words, it makes no sense for the commissioner of major league baseball to award a ballplayer a World Series Championship Baseball Ring on the first day of training camp. It would feel unearned. It would have no meaning. Instead, we allow the player to play, to compete over a long, challenging season so that he can *earn* the right to wear the championship ring, overcoming adversity every step of the way.

My friends, that is the *only* way that someone can truly appre-ciate what it means to be a champion.

The Creator certainly has the power to furnish us with endless joy and answers, but *ultimate* joy comes from being the Cause of our own fulfillment. That is to say that when we behave like the Creator, we create JOY!

So we said: God, please give us that opportunity!

In other words, God originally said: LET THERE BE LIGHT!

We responded and said: LET THERE BE DARKNESS, SO WE CAN EARN OUR OWN LIGHT!

The Creator said, "Okay."

And then: Poof!

BIRTH OF A COSMOS

In that one moment, God literally pulled back and withdrew a tiny portion of His infinite energy, which Kabbalah calls Light. This withdrawal created an explosion known as the Big Bang, which produced this universe, a tiny dark arena where we could play the Game of Life. This game consists of asking questions and finding the answers through our own hard work. That's the whole story. The universe in a nutshell. If you think life is any more complicated than this, you are mistaken, according to Kabbalah.

That tiny arena is what we experience as our vast universe. Here we perceive nothing but constant questions, chaos, and conflict, interwoven with rare moments of happiness. There's good reason for this. If we could reach the hidden World of

Answers with our five senses, we would find every single answer in an instant. There would be no challenge, and that would be no different from our original existence, when the Creator gave us everything, all at once. Put another way, a treasure hunt is not much fun if the treasure has a neon sign pointing right at it. We want the joy of the hunt, and the physical universe gives us that opportunity. The real treasures of life, the answers to every question we can pose, are hidden from view by design.

THE DELETE BUTTON

You and I asked the Creator to conceal the World of Answers. And, the Creator complied by putting up a curtain. This curtain, or filter, is our five senses. These senses have a difficult time sensing anything beyond the physical world around us. Now follow this next idea closely. Not only did we ask for the World of Answers to be hidden from us physically, we also asked for the World of Answers to be hidden from our conscious awareness.

Specifically, we asked for our memory banks to be completely erased so that we would have no recollection whatsoever of true reality, the World of Answers, and the meaning of life. With our memories deleted, we could now play this game of life and find answers through hard work, trial and error, and individual effort.

THE POWER AND PURPOSE OF DOUBT

In addition to erasing our memory banks and hiding true reality behind a curtain, the Creator planted another force into humankind. This energy was implanted into our very DNA, into every cell of our body, and it expresses itself in our rational mind.

This force is called Doubt. It is also called the Adversary.

Kabbalists also call it Ego.

We are programmed to doubt every single idea presented in this book. Moreover, we are programmed to doubt the very idea that we are programmed to doubt. For thousands of years, we doubted the possibility of achieving everlasting happiness, which is why everyone tried to grab as much for themselves as possible. We didn't buy into the fact that our Creator could dish out all the joy that we could possibly want. In other words, we made God way too small, which in turn made us very greedy. This greed, this desire for immediate gratification without any awareness of another reality waiting for us behind the curtain, is the reason history is littered with hostility, war, and genocide.

We doubted truth. We were skeptical about the existence of the Creator. We were so skeptical that many of us fabricated new ideas about what God is, and we got it all wrong.

Many of us don't really believe that there is a hidden spiritual reality. We doubt that something exists beyond death. We're unsure that order and meaning lie beneath all the random chaos. We doubt that this world is actually an illusion and that a world of paradise is in our destiny.

The reason for all this doubt is to ensure that we *earn* all the answers that we seek and the endless joy that is destined to be ours. Doubt is an indication to us that it is time to dig deeper, because hidden behind the curtain of doubt is a yearning for truth that originates at the level of our soul. And when we begin to seek truth, we will inevitably find ourselves closer to the Light of the Creator, because the Creator *is* Truth.

Unfortunately, our formidable Adversary called Doubt, or Ego, has gotten the best of us for thousands of years. Still, some people have managed to escape the vortex of doubt and see beyond the sensory filter that is physical reality. You might have heard about them. They are called kabbalists.

PEOPLE OF TRUTH

There have been individuals throughout the ages who were able to find the answers hidden behind the curtain. Moses did. Jesus did. The prophet Muhammad did. Buddha did. These great souls knew that the answers to life's questions did not dwell here in the material, physical world. These spiritual giants were able to pull back the curtain and enter into that higher reality.

But you know what happened? When they tried to share the truths they had found there, our innate doubts and greed rejected what they had to say. Even worse, we misinterpreted their words and distorted their teachings to further serve our own self-interest. Instead of digging deeper, we rejected truth out of hand.

And when we reject truth, we create lies. And I'm sorry to say that the lies we conjured were quite successful.

THE ART OF THE LIE

According to Kabbalah, the most effective lie always contains a kernel of truth. That's the secret to telling a good whopper. Many negative people throughout history understood this technique very well, indeed.

These ego-driven individuals took the intrinsic truths taught by the great sages and twisted them in order to serve their own misguided interests. The result? The birth of religion and, with it, all of the destructive by-products of religion.

Let's be honest. More blood has been spilled under the guise of religion than any other single cause. Over the last few thousand years, we have committed genocide in the name of Jesus. We have murdered in the name of Moses. We have massacred in the name of Muhammad. We have battled in the name of Buddha. We have hurt one another all in the name of these great leaders who taught nothing but love and kindness toward others.

Despite the often tragic consequences of religion, there have been those who craved a closer connection to God so intensely that they chose to overlook the corruption. They falsely believed there was no other option, thereby putting themselves into a corner. This led to unquestioning adherence to organized religions that did little to benefit humanity. The original message was lost under heaps of convoluted religious doctrine. What was that original message?

Love thy neighbor as thyself.

That was the original message God bestowed upon Moses, upon Jesus; this was all God asked of us. God loved us, and all he wanted was for us to do the same for one another. But it didn't take long for this divine guidance to become soiled by those seeking power, not love.

Throughout history kabbalists tried to expose the corruption of religion and empower people with tools to help them find their own answers. In response, the religious establishment subjected these truth-seekers to brutal persecution. If you have read my other books, you know that generations of kabbalists, including my own family, experienced this hate first-hand as they tried to share Kabbalah with the world.

Now, it would be easy to feel sad and embittered at this point in the story. But my goal is not to rile you up, but rather to offer you another way. By reading the pages of this book, you are opening yourself to a lasting and loving truth that has the ability to eliminate hate and intolerance on this planet forever.

THE PROMISE OF SCIENCE

Not surprisingly, many rational people driven by logic rejected religion by pointing out its lies, manipulations, and hypocrisies. For these people, it was plain to see that any "truth" that espoused intolerance and hate was a lie in sheep's clothing. In response, they invested their energy, their hopes and dreams in the physical laws of the natural world. After all, the physical world seemed to offer an objective reality, one that was not open to nearly as much interpretation as religion.

But this approach left out a critical component of the equation: a Creator. After all, if we can't observe any force working behind the scenes, then there must not be one. This led to the birth of science and atheism. When a scientist discovered a universal truth, be it the law of gravity or the workings of quantum mechanics, it was like finding one more piece of a puzzle. The problem was that science defined that puzzle in a very finite way. Science wasn't wrong; it was merely incomplete, since it failed to take into account the divine workings of the ultimate puzzle-maker, God.

But this was ignored because every scientific discovery offered a quick shot of ego-boosting gratification, and the number of disciples of science and technology grew.

SCIENCE AND RELIGION

Do you see what is wrong with this picture? Both organized religion and science have kept civilization imprisoned in a World of Questions. The kinds of answers science provides us cannot answer the most important questions, those that relate to the meaning of life. They do not tell us why we hate, why we divorce, why we hurt, why we fail, or why we are here. Science tells us *how* things work, but never addresses the question of *why*. Proven scientific laws might be correct in their physical context. But we get into trouble when we attempt to understand the universe using *only* the lens of science.

Religion, as we know it, also fails to answer any questions of substance. When we question why we perform various rites and rituals, the answer often given is: *because it is written*. When you ask religion why evil exists, or why tragedy strikes good people, the answer given is: *God works in mysterious ways*.

The bottom line is this: answers that would lead us to a life overflowing with meaning and happiness have eluded us throughout the centuries—despite the fact that they have been there all along.

LOST WINDOWS OF OPPORTUNITY

Many people mistakenly believe Moses was given a religion on Mount Sinai. Not true. God gave Moses a technology to access the World of Answers so that humanity could put an end to hatred and stop destruction and death once and for all. That technology is called Kabbalah. The two tablets that Moses held were merely powerful kabbalistic tools for helping us access the World of Answers. The two tablets were ignition keys that activated the infinite forces that comprise this hidden reality.

But what did religion do? Religion told us that Moses was given *commandments* on Mount Sinai. Ten, to be exact. That was clever, because who could question a commandment? A commandment, by definition, implies that you unquestionably tow the line, following along blindly. The truth of the matter is that the phrase *ten commandments* never appears in the original Hebrew Bible. The correct phrase is the ten utterances, and kabbalists told us 2,000 years ago that it refers to the unseen World of Answers made up of ten hidden dimensions, which we'll discuss a bit later. That's what Moses achieved on Sinai. He plugged the world into that blissful unseen reality.

Being plugged into this hidden world means you get truthful answers. And the truth frequently hurts. It's easier to hold onto our ego and believe falsehoods than to surrender our ego and embrace painful truths. Harry Truman once said: "I don't give them hell. I just tell them the truth and they think it's Hell."

This is what happened on Mount Sinai. The Israelites preferred to hang on to their selfishness rather than face the truth. They were not yet ready to receive the Tablets, the technology of Kabbalah, because it meant they would have to acknowledge their egotism. They would have to eradicate that over-sized ego in order to find the answers to life's questions and the true joys of life.

In fact, the Israelites complained about Moses, questioning his intentions every chance they could. They went so far as to accuse Moses of trying to murder them in the desert. This is not my opinion; it is stated quite clearly in the Bible.

A SECOND CHANCE

From the nature of his teachings it is easy to see that Jesus was also a kabbalist. Like Moses, he tried to enlighten the world so that individuals could know and understand the love of the Creator personally. All of his teachings, all of the key concepts found in Christianity, are found in the ancient books of Kabbalah. Historically we know that Jesus never intended to found a new religion. He also never intended to follow the so-called religion of Judaism as we understand it today. Like the great Patriarchs that walked before him, Jesus was a student of the universal wisdom given to Abraham and Moses, and a student who was killed for trying to reveal these provocative truths to the world.

Once again, this is not just my opinion. I am sharing what the ancient kabbalists have to say on this subject. By the way, it was no easy task finding this information. When I requested copies of a particular text that revealed many secrets about Jesus and Kabbalah, it was sent with some pages missing that coincidentally happened to be the ones I was seeking. Nonetheless, after years of wrangling, we were finally able to retrieve most of the missing pages. I will now share with you what I found in the following passages.

According to Abraham Abulafia, a great 13th century kabbalist, all peoples of this world are interconnected as one. We are all children of the Divine. There is no right or wrong religion or one way to the Divine. But humanity must be unified!

According to Abulafia, peace—true peace, lasting peace, peace for all the peoples of the world—will only come about when the three major peoples of the world—Christians, Muslims, and Israelites—recognize they are one. They have operated as a dysfunctional family for twenty centuries, and the result has been bloodshed beyond human imagination. When these three siblings finally realize that they are, in fact, brothers, and that all of their sacred teachings, including the Torah, Quran, and New Testament, are really saying the same thing, joy beyond imagination will become our new reality. Sadly, kabbalists throughout history were slaughtered for uttering such ideas.

UNITY THROUGH DIVERSITY

Although individual people have differences on the surface, humanity as a whole is like a perfectly healthy human body that consists of many different organs, each performing a unique function for the larger purpose of maintaining a happy and healthy body. A heart is never meant to become a liver. What's more, all the diverse organs of the body—from a brain to a kidney—are made up of the same atoms. So beneath the diversity lies a stunning oneness.

Likewise, according to Kabbalah, civilization consists of one body, the body of humanity. Each group, be it Islamic, Christian, Israelite, Buddhist, or Hindu, for example, is merely an organ of the body of man, serving its own unique function to help create one healthy and happy civilization.

This metaphor of a body and its parts representing the intricate workings of humanity brings us back to the notion that the physical and the spiritual are inextricably intertwined. In fact, the scientific laws that govern this physical world support these spiritual ideas that kabbalists have known about for centuries. For example, the discovery of atoms proved that we are all made up of the same stuff—a discovery that surprised many but only confirmed what great spiritual leaders had always known—the souls of humanity are indeed one.

Conversely, events that we might perceive as divine miracles seem to defy science, but in reality, they simply support the notion that there are forces in this universe that we are only beginning to understand from a scientific perspective. The field of quantum physics, which examines the behavior of atomic particles, is an excellent example of this. Scientists are beginning to gain insight into a world in which particles behave in ways that were never seen before.

The beauty of Kabbalah is that it recognizes that the miraculous and science are one and the same. Kabbalah and science speak the same language and describe the same reality; they are two sides of one coin.

At the core, we are all made up of the same spiritual atoms. We are all sparks of the Divine. But our doubts and greed (which were programmed into us so that we could work at discovering these truths) created tension and conflict between brothers, villages, cities, and nations. When we find the World of Answers, all these uncertainties are removed. All our questions are addressed. All our prayers are answered.

According to Kabbalist Abraham Abulafia, the Names of God and the wisdom of Kabbalah can reunite all the peoples of the world, regardless of their faith, by weeding out corruption and revealing the elegant and profound spiritual unity that lies at the heart of all the world's major religions.

So stop blaming God for all the world's misfortune.
Stop blaming God for the existence of evil and darkness.
Stop saying "God works in mysterious ways" when you ponder why suffering and evil is all around us.

You wanted it. You demanded it. You just forgot that you did. And the reason you forgot was so you could discover the truth for yourself.

Are you ready to get a taste of it?

CHAPTER FOUR
QUESTIONS *AND* ANSWERS

YOU SAID YOU WANTED THE TRUTH

The reality of the situation is that this book can send you on the path to finding Truth, but the answers do not reside in the black and white print before you. The answers emerge from within you when you use the tools of Kabbalah over and over again. That being said, I know that you have some heavy questions on your mind if you are reading this book, and you won't feel content until you get some answers.

So we are going to answer the toughest of all questions, questions that have been asked by philosophers, rabbis, priests, atheists, Muslims, Christians, and Israelites throughout human history. More importantly, we are going to answer those questions point blank. But remember that these answers are just words in print. Your mind will do its best to try to reconcile these words with what it thinks it knows.

Needless to say, your ego will be on high alert. That's okay for now. It's a beginning. By simply admitting that we need help locating the answers to life, we are removing just a bit of ego. And, when we begin to shed ego, we begin to open ourselves to the World of Answers, our true home. Real knowing—real comprehension—takes practice. In the next chapter, we'll discuss ways we can practice true knowing by using the 42-Letter Name, but for now, let's appease the intellectual side.

Q & A

Q: Where is God?

A: Right here. God is in you. God is around you. The only reason you cannot experience the full power of God's Light is because it is hidden behind a curtain. But the good news is that this curtain cannot diminish God's power. Think of it like this: if you were to cover a brightly shining lamp with several layers of cloth, the room would grow progressively darker. But the original light of the lamp would never change. Never. Like the light of the lamp, God's Light is always there, shining brilliantly, and you always have access to it.

Q: What kind of behavior places a curtain over God's Light?

A: Ego. Being reactive. Each time a human being reacts to ego, a curtain is placed over the lamp. Fortunately, every time a human being overcomes ego, a curtain is removed. Keep in mind that the Light of God never changes. It remains constant. You have the free will to either remove curtains and bring more Light into your world, or add curtains and increase the darkness. This is why it makes no sense to blame God for the evil in our world. Evil is merely the lack of Light caused by curtains we hang, which diminish God's Light. Only you can take down the curtains to reveal the full intensity of Light that is always shining. When all the curtains are removed, the new reality on Earth will be paradise.

Q: If God loves us, why doesn't God take down the curtains for us?

A: Imagine yourself as a small child. You're playing Hide and

Seek. The object of the game is to find your friends. Finding your friends is the most enjoyable part; it's the reason you're playing the game. Imagine counting to ten, turning around and finding all your friends standing there, right in front of you. You win! But was it fun? Not in the least. Pleasure only becomes possible when your friends hide. The effort of finding them is what makes the game enjoyable.

Life works the same way.

When the souls of humanity were originally created, happiness and Light were standing right in front of us. We asked God to hide everything so that we could experience the joy of finding it. We wanted to be the Cause of our joy.

Q: Why religion?
A: Religion, as we understand it, is a corruption of the truth. God originally gave humanity specific tools to eradicate ego, layer by layer, so that we could discover His Light for ourselves. These tools were books and scrolls of wisdom that had the power to banish ego when used properly. However, our Adversary, our Ego, sabotaged this effort by transforming this simple technology into religion, with all its traditions and dogma. So, instead of eradicating ego, the technology now fueled and expanded the ego, producing self-righteousness, arrogance, vanity, and pride.

The kabbalists say the Bible offers us a choice: we can either use the power concealed in its letters and verses to cure us of self-centeredness and conceit, or we can use the Bible to create more of the same egotism. Likewise, Kabbalah says the Torah is either a connection to the World of Answers or an addictive drug. Guess what? You have the free will to determine which one you choose.

Q: Why are there so many spiritual texts to choose from?

A: The Creator recognizes that we all live under varying circumstances; each nation, each individual has a different spiritual and physical makeup, just as each part of the body has a different function and different needs. Therefore, what might speak to one person might not have the same impact on another. For this reason, the Creator gave the people of the world several technologies for connecting to the World of Answers. These include the Quran, the Torah, the New Testament, the Upanishads, and the doctrines of Buddhism. This makes the ultimate truth accessible to everyone, since it is concealed inside each of these spiritual doctrines.

At the same time that the myriad of texts makes the hunt to discover God's truth challenging, the challenge makes it infinitely fulfilling. Remember that we have chosen to earn our joy; it is only through *earnership* that we connect to the World of Answers and access the Truth.

Q: Don't the various spiritual texts promote division among people?

A: They only create the illusion of division, and that is by design. By revealing only a portion of the truth to each group of people, the Creator fostered the illusion of difference. This leaves mankind the free will to choose to work together to discover the real truth—that beneath diversity there is unity.

Kabbalah likens this to the truth concerning sunlight. Sunlight is actually white. However, when it is divided up into its various frequencies, we see the seven primary colors of the rainbow— *red, orange, yellow, green, blue, indigo*, and *violet*. It is only when all of the different colors join together that we have the brilliance that is sunlight.

With this metaphor in mind, suppose you had seven groups of people each in possession of one color from the rainbow. You had the Red Religion, the Blue Religion, the Green Religion, and so on. Each group believes it has the perfect color, and they argue for centuries over who is right. Of course, they are all right. Each of the seven groups is holding a piece of the truth. But there is a higher truth, <u>one</u> ultimate truth about the color of light. That truth is the color white, which contains all seven colors!

White light contains <u>all</u> the joy we seek. But we only find it when we unite with the rest of humanity, when all the peoples of the world share their wisdom with each other in harmony and mutual respect.

Q: Why does death exist?
A: Every soul comes into this world to find answers. Every soul comes into this world to find ultimate happiness. To make this a worthwhile challenge, the soul wears a costume called ego. This masquerade not only conceals your true identity from others, but it hides your true self from you!

Every person is given an average of 70 years to remove the ego, to conquer selfishness, and to find the truth about life. This was what the path of spirituality and Kabbalah was all about. Every time we listen to our ego, and we react and behave with intolerance, anger, fear, selfishness and resentment, we dim the light of our soul. A curtain is placed over the Light that shines within us. When those curtains become dense enough, the Light is finally blocked out completely and the body loses contact with the soul, the true you. The soul is still shining, but the body is disconnected from its life force. This leads to death. The soul now ascends into the spiritual world and awaits a new body to try to win the game of life once again.

That's one reason for death. Here's another. Death also serves as a cleansing agent. It's a purification process that removes all the curtains that we have built up. When we finally remove the ego from our being once and for all, we will achieve immortality. When there is no ego there will be no curtains left to dim the Light of our soul. Now the body and soul will live forever.

Q: Why is there suffering?
A: There are two ways to rid a human being of ego. Suffering is one. Spiritual transformation is the other. The body hates pain. Each time you feel pain, it weakens your ego. Remember 9/11? The world felt enormous pain, sadness, and shock. But at the same time, we suddenly felt enormous unity, a great love for our neighbors. Republicans got along with Democrats. Strangers felt like our friends.

Pain has that strange effect on us. But isn't that a foolish way to learn our lessons in life? Even worse, most people suffer for a lifetime and still fail to learn the lessons they were born into this life to learn. Only a few weeks after 9/11, firemen and cops were fighting on the streets of New York. Republicans were back bickering with Democrats. We had lost that loving feeling! When we don't understand <u>why</u> a tragic event occurs (to rid us of ego and self-interest), then the ego quickly reasserts itself.

What happens when we don't grasp the purpose of suffering? We believe we are victims, that life is random, and that we're plagued by misfortune. This is all the work of the Adversary.

Q: Why is there such a thing as *time*?
A: For every action there is an equal reaction somewhere down the line. According to Kabbalah, the interval that separates cause and effect, action and reaction, is called time, therefore Kabbalah defines time as *the distance between cause and effect.*

Why does time exist? Consider the house training of a small puppy. Every time the puppy leaves a yellow puddle on the carpet, a newspaper immediately smacks the pup across the snout. Pretty soon the pup stops leaving puddles on the carpet. This is an example of a very short cause and effect process. There was an action (peeing on the carpet) and an immediate reaction (whack!). The puppy quickly transforms its behavior.

If God took a newspaper and whacked us every time we behaved egotistically or left a mess in someone else's life, we would transform pretty quickly. But there would be no free choice in the matter. Time delays the whack, which creates the illusion of injustice. Now we seem to get away with our crimes and misdemeanors. And kindness doesn't seem to pay off.

It can take us a lifetime to finally raise our consciousness, raise our vision, and deepen our insight so that we can begin to connect the dots in life. As we become wiser, spiritually speaking, we begin to see that all of our actions are like seeds being planted. It might take minutes, months, decades, or lifetimes, but sooner or later the repercussions of our actions will blossom. For those who have the wisdom to perceive the process of cause and effect that underlies all events, life appears elegant, purposeful, and well-ordered. Every moment becomes an opportunity to invest shrewdly in a future that bears the most delicious fruits.

For those who fail to connect the dots, seeing themselves merely as victims, life is chaotic, random, and filled with misfortune. Existence is a crapshoot, a nightmare where the dice keep turning up sevens!

Kabbalah also defines time as *mercy*. Why mercy? Suppose you commit a terrible deed, motivated by pure, unadulterated selfishness. The cause and effect principle dictates that at some point in the future, a mean and nasty effect of equal measure is going to suddenly appear in your life. Time delays the consequence. It puts repercussions on temporary hold. This is mercy. It means that before judgment strikes, you are given a chance to redirect the payback away from yourself! You can reprogram the missile so that it misses its intended target. How? Through transformation.

If you make the effort to change a particular part of your nature, the specific aspect of your ego that caused you to commit your selfish action in the first place, judgment will be unable to find you. You are now a different person. The missile of judgment cannot find its target because the original target no longer exists. This is the reward of internal change. Each little bit of change that we achieve removes judgments that are headed our way. Of course, there are many aspects to our ego, and there are many effects waiting to appear in our life. But the more we change, the more judgments we avoid.

Thank goodness for time. Just don't waste it!

Q: Are we nearing the end of the world?
A: According to Kabbalah, the universe is over 15 billion years old. But human consciousness, which is defined as the free will to effect spiritual transformation, is 5,767 years old as this book is being written. This date correlates to the years 2006-2007 in the western calendar.

Basically, the world as we know it is destined to last 6,000 years. Of these, 5,767 years have already elapsed. That means there are only 233 years left. After the 6,000 years have passed, there will be 1,000 years of paradise on earth, a time known as the seventh millennium. This paradise includes the end of death, the end of suffering, and the birth of eternal fulfillment and joy. After the 1,000 years of paradise, the world will move into an even higher dimension of fulfillment. Time, as we know it, will come to an end. Happiness will become a never-ending reality so blissful, so euphoric, that it is beyond our present intellectual capacity to understand or appreciate it.

Q: If we are destined for paradise, why do we need to change our reactive behaviors?
A: The ancient sages of Kabbalah assure us that by the time the sixth millennium ends and the seventh millennium begins, the Adversary will be defeated. That's the good news. The bad news is that if our present way of life continues on its course for another 233 years, the removal of the human ego will involve extreme torment and suffering. In fact, the final 233 years will make all the previous horrors of humanity look tame by comparison. The *Zohar* describes this time period with two very specific words: *Woe* and *Blessed*. The term *Woe* refers to the disease, war, terror, and ruination of the environment that we are experiencing first-hand as we enter these final years.

Fortunately, you and I will be given ample opportunity to become one of the *Blessed*. Right here. How? By proactively using the tools of Kabbalah, along with our own particular spiritual beliefs, to banish ego and self-centeredness from our nature. During this time of intense pressure and pain, we will come to recognize the value and wisdom of treating everyone with human dignity—including our rivals at work, strangers on the street, and our perceived enemies on the other side of the globe. When a critical mass of people in our world achieves this objective, the suffering ends—and the joy begins!

Q: What is that critical mass, that magic number?

A: No one knows. Some kabbalists say it's ten people—ten people who truly learn to love each other unconditionally, no matter what; ten people who actively remove all traces of selfishness from their nature. Just ten people could transform the world and benefit all of humanity, according to many kabbalist sages. Clearly this hasn't happened yet. Perhaps the magic number is 100. Perhaps it is 100 million. Whatever that number may be, Kabbalah says each person who commits himself or herself to the path of personal transformation will experience blessings, protection, and good fortune despite the chaos and strife that rage all around them. I think you might agree that changing our selfish ways is well worth that promise! But how do we begin to find our footing on this transformative path? You might have guessed it—the answer lies in the number 42!

CHAPTER FIVE

AN ANSWER TO OUR PRAYERS

THE 42-LETTER NAME OF GOD

What's so remarkable about the number 42? We touched on some fun points earlier, but now it's time to dig much deeper. The *Zohar* tells us that the 42-Letter Name of God represents 42 forces of energy. When 50 other specific forces are added to the 42 letters, these 92 elemental forces create and maintain the entire universe. The *Zohar* puts it this way:

"Those 42 letters by which this world was created, together with the supernal letter HEI (which is 50) from the Holy Name of God, equal 92."

Two-thousand years later, it turns out the *Zohar* was correct. Science tells us that there are precisely 92 different atoms, which, according to cosmologist Arthur Young, "provides the alphabet of nature."

These 92 atoms combine in various ways to produce everything we know (and even those things we have yet to discover).

The Prayer of the Kabbalist, the secret 42-Letter Name of God, gives us the ability to change the world—to change our lives—at the most fundamental level of this reality. The *Zohar* says that not only can we modify the building blocks of the atom—the electron, proton, and neutron—but the prayer of the 42-Letter Name influences the actual forces that *create* electrons, protons, and neutrons. Get the idea? This prayer goes to the cause of all causes, to the ultimate source of reality, and this is exactly where the World of Answers resides!

The only technology capable of connecting us to this ultra-microscopic dimension, this hidden realm, uses an ancient medium: letters. Letters are the link. Letters are the interface. Letters are the bridge between the physical and the spiritual, between intangible thought and tangible expression (i.e. language).

Yes, this *is* a bit abstract, but in actuality it's as easy as ABC—literally! A, B, C are letters! And we are dealing with the Aramaic language, which is the language of Jesus, the language of the Great Kabbalist Rav Shimon bar Yochai, and the language of the *Zohar*. Remember our ignition key analogy? Just as the unique shape of a key is the mechanism by which you open a door, or fire up your car engine, the unique shapes of the Names of God are the mechanism by which we open the gates of heaven and fire up the forces of creation.

It's now time to discover precisely how this magnificent technology operates, so we can start effecting change in our lives right now.

THE STRUCTURE OF THE NAME OF 42

Letters	Six words (read right to left)	Sephira	#
אבג יתץ	צְרוּרָה תַּתִּיר יְמִינְךָ גְּדוּלַת בְּכֹחַ אָנָּא tserura — tatir — yeminekha — gedulat — bekho'ah — ana	חסד Hesed	1
קרע שטן	קַבֵּל רִנַּת עַמְּךָ שַׂגְּבֵנוּ טַהֲרֵנוּ נוֹרָא nora — taharenu — sagvenu — amekha — rinat — kabel	גבורה Gevura	2
נגד יכש	נָא גִּבּוֹר דּוֹרְשֵׁי יִחוּדְךָ כְּבָבַת שָׁמְרֵם shomrem — kevavat — yihudekha — dorshey — gibor — na	תפארת Tiferet	3
בטר צתג	בָּרְכֵם טַהֲרֵם רַחֲמֵי צִדְקָתְךָ תָּמִיד גָּמְלֵם gomlem — tamid — tsidkatekha — rahamey — taharem — barkhem	נצח Netsah	4
חקב טנע	חֲסִין קָדוֹשׁ בְּרוֹב טוּבְךָ נַהֵל עֲדָתֶךָ adatekha — nahel — tuvekha — berov — kadosh — hasin	הוד Hod	5
יגל פזק	יָחִיד גֵּאֶה לְעַמְּךָ פְּנֵה זוֹכְרֵי קְדוּשָׁתֶךָ kedushatekha — zokhrey — peneh — le'amekha — ge'eh — yahid	יסוד Yesod	6
שקו צית	שַׁוְעָתֵנוּ קַבֵּל וּשְׁמַע צַעֲקָתֵנוּ יוֹדֵעַ תַּעֲלוּמוֹת ta'alumot — yode'a — tsa'akatenu — ushma — kabel — shav'atenu	מלכות Malchut	7
	(בלחש) בָּרוּךְ שֵׁם כְּבוֹד מַלְכוּתוֹ לְעוֹלָם וָעֶד: (silently) — barukh — shem — kevod — malkhuto — le'olam — va'ed		

The 42-Letter Name of God is arranged in seven lines, as described in the *Sefer Yetzirah*, also known as the *Book of Formation* or the *Book of Abraham*. Each of the seven lines has six words that are read from right to left.

7 x 6 = 42

The seven lines correlate to the seven days of the week. Now follow this next idea carefully: each word has its own ignition key. This is the *first letter* of each word. The moment your eyes make contact with that first letter the engines of creation fire up. Likewise, when you utter the letter during the recitation of the word, the ignition key turns and the engines roar louder. Contact between the eye and the letter, or the mouth and the letter, is the flashpoint that ignites the power of the prayer.

Before we learn how to recite each of these words, let's first understand what each of the seven lines offers us in the way of power, change, and control over our physical reality.

THE FIRST LINE

THE FIRST LINE – SUNDAY
ANA BEKHO'A<u>H</u> GEDULAT YEMINEKHA TATIR
TSERURA.
ALEF, BET, GIMEL, YUD, TAV, TSADI

The first line acts as the seed of the entire 42-Letter Name and the first word is the seed of the first line. So the first letter of the first word is the seed of the entire prayer. This is why the first line begins with the letter *Aleph. Aleph* is the first letter of the Hebrew alphabet, the original seed, the beginning of every-thing. This is very important.

Here, with the very first letter, we arrive at the source of cre-ation, and it is here where we can effect change at the DNA level of existence—the seed level. Kabbalists love seeds. They love the metaphor of trees. Why? A tree represents the many processes of life as it interacts with the larger world, on every level imaginable. Kabbalah says that in the event of sickness, if you can repair the original seed, specifically the DNA inside the seed, you immediately cure the entire tree. This is because you are addressing the root cause of the sickness. But if you are trying to repair a branch, a fruit or a leaf, it's already too late. You are dealing with the symptoms of disease. You are coping, and kabbalists refuse to cope. They are only interested in restoring.

With the very first letter of the 42-Letter Name of God you are beginning to heal your life at the seed level.

ELIMINATING TIME, SPACE, AND MOTION

Here's our problem in life: You have a dream. You set a goal. But then the waiting game begins. Why? Because there is one vital component that separates you from achieving your desired outcome. It is called *time*. It's also called *space*. (Einstein showed us that time and space were two sides of one coin, hence the term, *space-time continuum*.) This opening, this window of time, allows negative forces and obstacles to fill the empty space, which makes it far more difficult for you to accomplish your goal. You run up against interference patterns. Roadblocks. Friction. All these impediments delay the arrival of your fulfillment.

Your .... The Object of
Desire   Your Desire
(TIME & SPACE)

Imagine removing time from the equation. What if there was no space separating you from the fulfillment that you seek? The moment you desired something you would receive it instantly! *Wouldn't that be nice?* There would be no room for obstacles, mistakes, and misunderstandings.

This is precisely the purpose of the first line. Its six letters help tear down the walls of time and space. Time constricts. Space shrinks. Everything accelerates. Dreams come true faster. Goals are achieved in no time.

BUT KEEP IN MIND: You get what you ask for! So be careful.

Here are two tips to help you achieve the happiness that you crave:

TIP #1

BE CAREFUL NOT TO PRAY FOR THE WRONG THINGS

There are two ways to receive answers to your prayers. One is to pray on behalf of the ego—in other words, to indulge it. The second is to pleasure the soul, or to fulfill it. The choice is yours. Which of the two do you wish to please?

Here's the tip: When you gratify the ego, the joy will be intense and immediate. But there is a trade-off. The joy will only be temporary. Short and sweet. Not only that: every time you make the choice to pleasure your ego, you're passing up a chance at something much more valuable—something that you can't put your finger on, yet it has the ability to soothe your soul for the long haul. Let me explain.

Every day, life offers choices, which allow you to accumulate assets. These assets fall into two groups: the most valuable assets in the universe and assets that become valueless over the long term. The assets that lose their value consist of everything money can buy, and these items provide you with diminishing returns over time. The other set consists of all other assets. Here's a sample list. (Feel free to make your own list, or to add to this one.)

LIST ONE	LIST TWO
(WHAT MONEY CAN BUY)	(WHAT MONEY CANNOT BUY)
House	Home
Sex	Love
The Best Doctors	Health
The Best Psychiatrists	Peace of Mind
Freeloaders	Friends
Cars	Enjoyment
Beachfront house	Inner Peace and Security
Designer Clothes	Self-Worth
Wife or Husband	Soul Mate
Drugs	Fulfillment
Information	Wisdom
Power	Courage
Being Honored	Being Cared For

The Adversary will offer you a choice each and every day. Your job is to choose which asset you want to receive. That is your only choice. You can choose from List One or from List Two. Your ego's initial reaction—every time—will be to accept the offer from List One. But once you make your choice from List One, you grant the Adversary the power to take away an asset from List Two. It's not a fair trade-off, but it's one that we choose time and time again.

This is life. These are the irrefutable laws of human existence. You can deny them. You can choose not to accept them. That is your prerogative. That's free will in action. But it won't change anything. Every time you choose an asset from List One, the Adversary takes away something from List Two. Plain and simple.

By now you might have noticed that kabbalists are not a moralistic bunch. Kabbalists are not lording their ethical choices over other people. But kabbalists are sharp-witted investors. They've learned how to bet only on long-term investments that pay off handsomely.

They don't reject materialism because it's a noble thing to do. They don't turn away from the ego's choices because of a moralistic ideal. They simply see the wisdom in swapping worthless possessions for priceless wealth.

When you choose an item from List One, the Adversary plants the notion in your mind that you are a smart player. And you buy into it. It makes you feel good—for a moment. But now you know the truth. It's a sucker's bet.

So, again, be careful what you pray for. You might just get it.

Now, does this mean you should give up that plan to purchase a house, buy an expensive pair of Italian shoes, drive a nice car, and carry around an iPod? No, this is not what it means. Relax. No one is asking you to give up all your possessions, or go live on a mountain and become one with nature. That would be too easy, believe it or not. It's much tougher to live in this chaotic material world and earn true fulfillment.

If it is your intention to choose a home over a fancy house, the Light of the Creator, the World of Answers, will send you a home. But if it's your intention to have a big gadget-filled house to show off to your friends, you're trading away the possibility of a home and all of the warmth, love, and contentment that go along with it.

If you're obsessed with a person, you can ask God to make that person love you. But wouldn't you be better off asking God to bring you into a loving relationship? What might happen if you allowed God to handle the details of who your partner should be? Think about it.

Here's a secret that few people in organized religion know: *More than a calf wants to suckle, the cow wants to nourish its young.* In other words, God's desire to share pleasure and fulfillment with you is infinitely greater than your desire to receive it. In the end we are destined to have everything on *both* lists, and a lot more than that to boot. After all, the Creator's Light is infinite.

The key is discovering what defines real fulfillment and what constitutes temporary indulgence. When we *genuinely* choose List Two, when we truly dedicate our lives to achieving everything on List Two, then the items on List One are included, if they truly support what we want. We can have it all, so why ask for less? The difficulty is that we're just not used to thinking this way. It sounds simple. And it is. But it's not easy. It takes a lifetime to truly learn these lessons. I hope that this book and the tools set forth in it will allow you to start right now. Why waste another day searching for that which won't truly fulfill you?

Which brings me to Tip #2. (I promised you two tips, remember?)

TIP #2
NEVER ASK FOR ANYTHING ON LIST TWO!

"WHAT?
ARE YOU SERIOUS?"

THE WORLD OF ANSWERS IS RIGHT HERE

Yes, I am serious. You already have all the answers to your prayers. Everything on List Two is already here. Right now. Do you really think God would say "No" to your prayer to receive love, enjoyment, and peace of mind? God would never say no. Never!

Remember, God does *not* work in mysterious ways. God would never refuse a request to deliver happiness, health, and healing to a person in need. The reason our prayers go unanswered is because of the curtains we have created! Those curtains hide the answers and solutions that are already present, in the same way a blackout curtain can prevent sunlight from penetrating a room. The sunlight is always there. Always. But the curtain keeps the room darkened.

So what is List Two all about? And what in God's (42-Letter) Name are we to actually pray for?

IT ALL STARTS WITH INTENTION

Intention is the key to using the 42-Letter Name. Your intention should be to receive everything on List Two, but to do so you must focus your *actual* prayer on one of your nasty traits. You pray to remove a blockage. A curtain. An obstacle. A barrier. You meditate or pray to remove whatever has prevented your soul mate or financial comfort from coming into your life. Get it?

By meditating to eradicate your negative characteristics with the intention of receiving List Two, good things start flowing to you. Why? This next kabbalistic idea is brilliant, so pay attention: As you remove barriers (negative traits) from your nature, the first line of this ancient text automatically removes the barriers in the physical world. Time is shortened. Your dreams appear faster.

As we've seen, there is no concept of *time* in the Light that radiates from the Creator. God's Light is everywhere, all at once. This incredible divine Energy transcends all limitations of time, space, and motion. What does this mean for you? It means that the moment you let God's Light into your life, you'll receive instant rewards, which means no delays! In an instant, you'll witness an increase of all that the Light embodies—more joy, more love, and more happiness.

So, you now have to make a new list. Let's call this List Three.

CREATING LIST THREE

Take a moment and reflect. Honestly. Identify five personal traits of yours that you know are not nice. The more ruthlessly you identify these characteristics, the better results you will achieve. Now, because the Adversary skillfully blinds us to some of our nastier traits, you will almost certainly need the help of other people to help you find what you cannot perceive (or do not care to admit). According to Kabbalah, you only discover your worst negative traits by listening to the criticisms of others.

CHAPTER FIVE: AN ANSWER TO OUR PRAYERS

They are the messengers. Therefore, you must—*absolutely must*—ask your friends, and even some people you are not too fond of, to reveal three things that they cannot stand about you. Write those qualities down on a piece of paper.

Okay, you're getting there, but take a moment to try the following. Pick three people in your life. Person one should be a good friend. Person two should be a member of your family of origin. Person three should be someone who you really don't like, even an enemy.

Now, identify three unpleasant traits, three obnoxious characteristics, in each of these people. They may include laziness, jealousy, arrogance, or any other insufferable quality. Once you have identified these traits, put them at the very top of *your list*!

That's right. These are really the characteristics *you* need to work on! Kabbalah says everything that you see as being wrong in others is a direct reflection of your own self. It's like holding up a mirror. In fact, the physical world is a mirror by design. Remember, all truths are hidden from us, and our job is to find them. What better place to hide our own nasty attributes than within the people we interact with every day! This makes the task of finding our negative traits much more difficult and therefore much more rewarding once we discover the truth.

This new list is now your roadmap to the World of Answers. This is what you pray for: the absolute removal of all these traits from your character.

NO AGENDA

The first line of the 42-Letter Name of God also awakens unconditional love. By meditating on it, you can ignite the desire within you to offer the kind of love and kindness that has no strings attached. This first line helps you and the rest of the world to care for one another without any hidden agenda. The fact of the matter is that almost all charitable contributions and acts of friendship contain some form of ulterior motive. This keeps the curtains closed and the World of Answers out of our reach. When we share our love with others, on the other hand, the curtains fall away. Light shines in, and solutions arrive on our doorstep.

This means that we have to keep our unconditional love in circulation in order to receive more of the same. And in order to have a healthy circulatory system, we must have a healthy heart.

THE HEART OF THE MATTER

Despite the infinite love that exists in the hidden realm, we allow an immeasurable amount of hate to exist in this physical world. Conflict between people, tribes, villages, and civilizations has been a constant trademark of life on earth since the first humans formed clans. But these very conflicts, these differences among people, play a vital role in helping to bring true unity and peace to this world. How can our differences create unity? The *Zohar*, the most important book on Kabbalah, explains it with profound simplicity.

Consider a healthy human body. As we discussed earlier, the body is made up of diverse organs, each performing a unique function. The liver plays a different role than the heart. The kidney serves a different function than the lungs. But together, when they work in perfect harmony, they create one healthy human being.

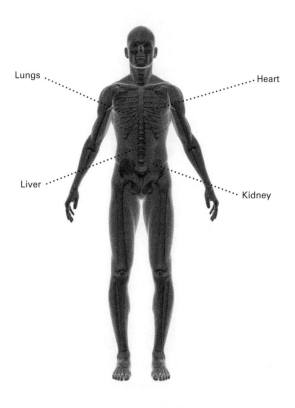

Each of the nations of this world, each group of people, whatever their particular beliefs, rituals, and customs may be, is a different organ in the *body of humanity*.

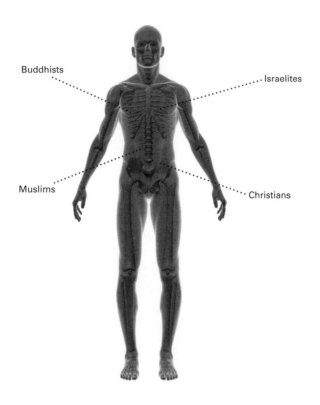

This is not poetry. This is the physics of reality. According to the *Zohar*, the Israelites play the role of the heart. In just a moment, I'll elaborate more on the definition of Israelite. But for the time being, all we need to remember is that the purpose of the heart is to nourish all organs with blood. If there is a lack of blood flow, heart attacks occur. Strokes happen. Gangrene sets in. Kabbalah says the 42-Letter Name of God is a vital artery that nourishes all the organs of the body (all the nations of the world) with blood (Light and Divine Energy). If there is hatred in the world, it's because Light is not flowing freely from the heart.

The first line of the 42-Letter Name of God is the specific artery that carries this Light to all nations, giving them a specific measure of spiritual nourishment. No nation can achieve perfection and lasting fulfillment on its own. We are all deeply and profoundly linked to one another in the same way that every organ and every cell of the body is inextricably linked. However, this truth was hidden away, at the time of Creation, so that we could discover this profound lesson on our own.

DEFINING ISRAELITE

You may have noticed that I did not use the word "Jew" to describe the role of the heart. I used the word "Israelite." An Israelite, according to the *Zohar*, is anyone who uses the path of Kabbalah to conquer all of his or her own egocentric characteristics and self-centered desires. In the Old Testament, there is a story about a man named Jacob who wrestles with an evil Angel related to Jacob's brother Esau. In the story, Jacob wrestles with the angel all night long. When Jacob finally defeats the angel, Jacob's name is changed to "Israel."

Like so many stories in the Old Testament, this story has an encoded meaning. Jacob is code for you and me. And the angel is a code for List Three! Each time we conquer a negative trait, we play the role of the heart. We pump blood, blessings, and Light to all the nations of the world. And when we conquer all the traits written down on List Three, we become an Israelite!

What if no one assumed the role of the heart, if no one dedicated their life to conquering List Three? There would be a lack of blood flow in the world, a lack of Light! And just as the body experiences a stroke due to lack of blood to the brain, humanity experiences war, genocide, drought, or famine when it suffers from a lack of Light flow to the nations of the world. This is because our physical world is a reflection of our spiritual condition.

So when you recite this first line of the 42-Letter Name, meditate hard; meditate with the conviction that you will share this Light with your enemies, with your friends, and with all the nations of the world. The energy that you are transmitting will warm their hearts, awaken their souls, and kindle love for you and everyone else in the world. Demand—and expect—miracles.

Not completely convinced yet? Rest assured that if this first line couldn't really achieve such a mind-blowing miracle, the kabbalists wouldn't have wasted a single second of their day on the 42-Letter Name of God. So tell your doubt to take a long walk, and just give it a try! Unconditional love will flow through the body and soul of every person on this planet each time you do. As more and more people continue to utilize this technology, the cumulative effect will be the systematic removal of hatred and ego from this world.

And it doesn't have to take a lifetime. This first line, because it removes space and time, brings the future to the here and now. It gives us an opportunity to accelerate the arrival of peace on earth! So what are you waiting for?

THE SECOND LINE

THE SECOND LINE – MONDAY
KABEL RINAT AMEKHA SAGVENU TAHARENU NORA.
KOF, REISH, AYIN, SIN, TET, NUN

This is one of the rare lines of the 42-Letter Name of God that literally spells something out, in this case using the first letters of each of the six words. They spell out the phrase:

KRA SATAN, which literally means *tear away Satan!*

No, it's not a line of dialogue from a horror movie. Nor is it the lunatic ravings of a religious fanatic. It's code. When Moses stood on Mount Sinai 3,400 years ago, he wrote on a scroll of parchment. We know these writings as the Old Testament, the Torah, or the first five books of the Bible. In that ancient text written some 34 centuries ago, we find the first use of the word *Satan* in its original Hebrew form.

Moses was not speaking about the horned devil we see in comic books or low-budget feature films. The precise English translation of the Hebrew Satan is "The Adversary." This Adversary is a real phenomenon that you experience every day of your life. You just don't know it. For instance, you make a commitment to lower your carbohydrate intake in your diet. A little later on, your craving for carbs amps up while another voice inside your head says, "Oh, go ahead. A few carbs never hurt anyone. Why not restart your diet on Monday?"

The voice that just sabotaged your true intention is the Adversary. It's not you. In fact, it hides the real you. The real you wants to be healthy and at a comfortable weight. But the Adversary would prefer that you continue to be a slave to your whims and cravings. That's because when you are occupying your mind with the next food fix, connecting to God's Light becomes a mere afterthought.

The Adversary is the Ego—the reactive, impulsive aspect of every human being. The Adversary was created to hide the real you so that the task of uncovering the Light would be challenging and therefore worthwhile and fulfilling.

YOUR ONE AND ONLY PROBLEM

None of this would be a problem, except for one thing: You believe the ego is you. You believe the Adversary's thoughts and impulses are yours. And the moment you believe that, it becomes true. You and the Adversary become one. Now the ego controls your life. You make promises to yourself and then you break those promises. You know you shouldn't do or say certain things and you go right out and do them anyway. You know you need to do certain things but you don't follow through on them—*even though you want to!*

This is why life is filled with so many ups and downs. When we listen to the ego, it gives us temporary rewards and immediate gratification. Life appears to be going our way. But sooner or later we are forced to confront the consequences of our ego-centric actions. Worse, when these repercussions finally appear, that same devious ego tells us that it's just a random occurrence and an unlucky event. And we buy it. We accept that life is chaotic, a sea of unforeseeable events, filled with misfortune. We have lost touch with our true selves. And the Ego, the one and only Adversary, will now do everything in its power to keep us from the truth and prevent us from connecting to the World of Answers.

How do we rid ourselves of the Adversary? We need to tear him out of our consciousness, out of every cell in our body. He is a curtain that conceals our true self. Tear away the curtain that blocks out the sunlight of our true selves and suddenly the world is completely transformed. Tear away the ego from your mind and your body and suddenly the True You will shine brightly!

This is the objective of the second line of the 42-Letter Name. It rips away all the Adversary's curtains, but not without asking something of you. First you must identify (and therefore admit to) the specific egocentric traits that you want to remove. The harder it is to admit to them, the greater the amount of Light this process will bring into your life.

CLOSING OPEN GATES

Did you ever try to block out all sunlight in a room during the day? It's practically impossible. Somehow a sliver of light always seems to penetrate the room.

Kabbalah calls these openings *gates*, and sees them as openings for the unwanted intruder. The same way sunlight, by its very nature, is relentless in its effort to illuminate a room, our Adversary is ruthless in his desire to take control over our behavior and life. No matter how many ways we try to block out his influence, somehow the Adversary sneaks in. Even the smallest of infractions, the tiniest acts of ego, create new openings, which allow the Adversary access to our lives.

But this second line of the 42-Letter Name of God seals the gates shut. All the openings, fissures, gaps, and holes that exist within us are hermetically sealed when we meditate on this one line. Talk about a powerful weapon to have at our disposal!

SHUTTING DOWN THE ADVERSARY

There are only two states of existence for a human being:

1. Reactive

2. Proactive

There is nothing else. You are either one or the other.

The reactive state means just that: you react to everything around you.

- An insult infuriates you.
- A compliment boosts your self-esteem.
- A lost business deal angers you.
- A pay raise makes you happy.
- You're envious when your best friend experiences good fortune.

- You're tickled when you purchase a nicer car than your friend.
- Turbulence on an airplane scares the wits out of you.
- When the airplane seatbelt light turns back off, you immediately calm down and breathe a sigh of relief.

In all of the above situations, something external controlled your feelings. Something outside of yourself directly affected your emotions. Your states of happiness, fear, jealousy, and relief were all caused by external stimuli. You reacted. You were out of control. You were not the cause of your feelings; you were only an effect.

By contrast, when you are in a proactive state, life is not happening to you, but rather you are happening to life. You are the cause. You are the creator. You are revealing the happiness that is the true core of your being by the choices you are making. Nothing around you is dictating your emotional state.

According to the structure of reality and the laws that govern our existence, reacting is a very serious problem. Why?

CONNECTION VERSUS DISCONNECTION

According to Kabbalah, every time you react, you disconnect from the World of Answers and root yourself a little deeper in the World of Questions. Conversely, every time you are proactive, you immediately connect to the World of Answers. So no matter how frightening the news may be, no matter how pessimistic a situation may look, if you react to it with fear, worry, or doubt, you wind up in the World of Questions. If you under-stand—*truly* understand—how this game of life works, you rec-ognize that, by being proactive, you immediately connect to the World of Answers and an infinite wellspring of solutions becomes yours!

HOW TO TRANSFORM FROM REACTIVE TO PROACTIVE

How does one become proactive? That is the million-dollar question!

Every time you make a conscious effort to **resist** a reaction, no matter how justified that reaction may seem, you immediately connect yourself to the World of Answers. Why? The moment you resist a reaction you are being proactive. Resisting is the vehicle that takes you from reactive to proactive.

The key point here is this:

> *Even if you are justified in your reaction, unless you resist it, you disconnect from the World of Answers!*

Do you want to be right, yet completely disconnected from the World of Answers? Or would you prefer to be connected to the solutions that you seek, even if it means appearing wrong in the eyes of others or your own ego? We waste so much pre-cious energy proving our case, rationalizing our behavior, and winning our arguments, yet all the while our reactive responses are keeping us imprisoned inside a world of chaos. When we stop reacting, life transforms right before our eyes.

In case you hadn't noticed, the pressures of life, with its endless stream of annoyances, push all your buttons. And the closer people are to you, the more adeptly they do it. Life is like one giant trigger that ignites reactions within you all day long. Is it any wonder that your prayers seem to go unanswered? You are living life fully immersed in the World of Questions.

A SOLUTION

When it becomes just too darn difficult to resist a reaction, line two of our text helps shut the whole system down. The lever controlling your reactive system flips into the off position. We're not talking about suppressing your feelings here. This is about shutting down the entire reactive system, letting it all go. It's the difference between coping and curing. Suppression involves holding in all our reactions as we attempt to cope with chaos. It's a dangerous and ineffective strategy, because eventually you will blow. Line two creates a full-scale blackout of your egocentric power grid. All reactions come to a grinding halt, and you find yourself in a simple, serene state of proactive being.

THE POWER OF KNOWING: FORGETTING ALL YOUR LIMITATIONS

The Adversary has a powerful weapon that he uses against you. It is called uncertainty. It is also called apprehension, doubt, or "thinking small." You see, the Adversary skillfully creates the illusion that you are limited. Imagine a solid brick wall standing 20 feet away from you. Would you run straight into it with full force? Of course you wouldn't. But what if you knew ahead of time that the brick wall was really a soft sheet made of the finest Egyptian cotton and that it was merely painted to look like a brick wall? Your fear would vanish. You'd run toward it without hesitation.

That's life. The Adversary paints brick walls around every area of our life. All of our doubts, uncertainties, and self-imposed limitations are really the handicraft of our Adversary. He's a brilliant artist who paints convincing images of limits, borders, and impossibilities.

But it's all just an illusion. Everything is possible. *Everything.* But our own belief in the brick wall can become a self-fulfilling prophecy as we build walls in our mind to avoid growth and challenge, and to avoid pursuing our dreams. These perceived obstacles, which take the form of fear and doubt, begin in our mind but give way to the physical obstacles that tower over us in life. But the minute we forget about the obstacles in our head, the physical obstacles in life simply melt away.

Take for example a mother or father who has long dreamed of starting a home-based business in order to spend more time with the kids. The mental barriers, which arrive in the form of what-ifs, worst-case scenarios, and just plain anxiety, keep this person from taking any action. The thoughts playing in this individual's mind probably sound something like this:

- What if I can't make enough money to support my family?
- What if I can't stay motivated on the job without a structured work environment?
- What if I end up regretting leaving my current job?

These thoughts—these limited, incomplete images—are just one of the Adversary's effective techniques for prompting you to let go of your dream and say goodbye to possibility. Remember that he wants you locked in fear and disconnected from the World of Answers, a world where possibility and hope abound. If the Adversary allowed you to connect to this world, then he would cease to exist in the face of such splendid Light and optimism.

That means as soon as you recognize fear and doubt for what they really are, you rid yourself of the Adversary's pull and you open yourself up to everything the Light has to offer. Your path becomes clearer, tasks become less challenging, and your motivation and energy to move forward on your dream increase by leaps and bounds. In other words, the brick walls you previously erected give way to soft, accommodating sheets.

WRIGHT OR WRONG

For thousands of years, flying through the air was a brick wall. It was impossible—that is, until the Wright brothers came along. These two crafty brothers proved that our thinking was not just limited, but plain wrong. In fact, every technological advancement, scientific breakthrough, and medical discovery was once considered impossible until someone decided to forget all the reasons why it wouldn't work and charge through the brick wall.

Line two of this ancient text helps you to ignore all the reasons something can't be accomplished and begin to dream boldly. With this line, you start believing in your ability to achieve anything your heart desires. But it doesn't stop there. Your certainty in yourself and in your dream continues to increase until you *know* you can achieve anything, instead of just believing it. And when you know something to be absolutely true, nothing can ever stop you from achieving it. Nothing.

Through the power of line two, you awaken true certainty. Then you rise from *belief* to the all-powerful consciousness of *knowing*!

THE THIRD LINE

THE THIRD LINE – TUESDAY
NA GIBOR DORSHEY YIHUDEKHA KEVAVAT SHOMREM.
NUN, GIMEL, DALET, YUD, KAF, SHIN

The first three letters of this line (**NUN**, **GIMEL**, **DALET**) open the door to true financial and spiritual prosperity. Notice that I said financial *and* spiritual prosperity; this is because these two concepts go hand in hand. But before we can truly comprehend what this means, we need to examine the places from which financial abundance flows.

There are two sources of financial good fortune in our world: the Adversary and the World of Answers. Both sources are like banks that continually lend you money throughout your life. The Ego, the Adversary, leads you to believe that you own your money and that you earned it all by yourself. But the fact of the matter is that all the money you make in life, all the assets you acquire, are really just loans. You do not take them with you when you leave this world.

Here's how it *really* works.

Both banks have unlimited amounts of cash on hand. And they each have their own unique system.

- **The Adversary's banking system is called THE REACTIVE BANK.**

- **The World of Answers' banking system is called THE PROACTIVE BANK.**

You draw money from The Reactive Bank every time you appease your ego by engaging in self-centered behavior to earn a buck. The Reactive Bank is only too happy to loan you money in this way, because the Adversary, your banker, charges interest on every loan you take out.

What is the interest? Turn back to page 58 and read all the items on List Two. These are your interest payments. You take payment in the form of self-serving rewards, while the Adversary takes away what you really wanted but failed to recognize.

When you decide to do your banking at The Proactive Bank, there is also interest charged. However, this interest does not come from List Two. The only interest you pay comes from your ego. That's right; you must cough up an egocentric trait as interest payment on the money you borrow. You must let go of reactivity. You must let go of selfish behavior. This is the requirement for taking money from The Proactive Bank.

That's it—the complete financial model on which life is based. Most of the people in the world have been drawing loans from The Reactive Bank and paying exorbitant interest rates in return, leaving these individuals feeling desperate and spiritually impoverished. Is it any wonder there is so much chaos in the world?

On a more personal level, is it any wonder parts of your life contain some happiness while other parts are filled with all kinds of troubles? The Adversary makes sure that you never connect the dots between your reactive behavior and your pain. The Adversary makes sure that you never know about the two banks, the loans, and all the interest payments. Even now he will work on you to question these words. "It's a clever metaphor, this whole idea of Reactive and Proactive Banks," he will tell you. But don't be fooled.

You work hard all day to earn a living. You slave all week to receive a paycheck. You hustle 24-7 to build and grow a business. All the success you receive, all the money you make, no matter how much or how little, it's all earned through your reactive nature. Why? The odds are you never understood that the rules you were living by were illusions. But now that you know the Adversary exists, now that you know both banks exist, you can start drawing prosperity from The Proactive Bank.

YOUR NEW PASSWORD

The first three letters of line three are your new password for the bank card you will use to draw money from The Proactive Bank. When you meditate upon this sequence of letters and you admit one of your egocentric habits or behaviors at the same time, you immediately withdraw spiritual currency, which translates into good fortune and financial blessings. When you demonstrate tolerant and kind behavior in your day-to-day life, when you surrender a reactive trait in business, with friends, or with your family, you are the biggest beneficiary. The more you bury your ego, the more riches you draw from The Proactive Bank, which (as you might have guessed) is just another name for the Light of the Creator.

But don't be misled. This sequence of letters is not a get-rich-quick formula—far from it. Kabbalah tells us that a person's financial state of affairs is based on karma. The amount of money you make depends on decisions you made long ago, perhaps even before this lifetime. But we all have the ability to transform our life, and that includes our existing financial situation. When we truly change and genuinely transform our reactive ways, we alter our destiny and change what was once unchangeable. This is called free will, and each of us has the free will to decide whether to withdraw cash from The Reactive Bank or The Proactive Bank in this lifetime. Remember that any pain, any discomfort, any misfortune, any lack that you might have in your life, is the result of having done your banking at the wrong financial institution. But when you meditate on the first three letters, you align yourself with the right lender and all that He represents. So, although these letters aren't a get-rich-quick scheme, the power that they possess opens the gate to infinite spiritual and financial abundance.

The mere fact that you are bringing this particular line of the 42-Letter Name of God into your life for the purpose of connecting to prosperity is a declaration that you want to start banking at The Proactive Bank. You are recognizing its existence. That is 90% of the battle.

THE POWER OF THE EMBRYONIC STATE

The third line of the 42-Letter Name starts with a bang and ends with a bang. That is to say that the last three letters of this line (**YUD**, **KAF**, **SHIN**) also contain tremendous powers. They have the ability to return every cell in your body back to its embryonic state, to purify and cleanse the cell, returning it to its normal healthy condition. We are talking about the spiritual version of stem cell therapy.

All cells start out as stem cells. These cells then take on specific identities, transforming into heart, liver, kidney, or brain cells. Over time, these cells become worn out and function less efficiently. But the last three words of this line have the power to bring cells back to their original and perfect state. When used each and every day, this meditation restores and rejuvenates damaged cells and repairs the broken parts of your life, too. How is healing at this level possible?

The answer is in the atom.

Positive and Negative Charges

When souls were created, **_receiving_** was their function. Receiving was their essence. Receiving was their purpose. After all, nothing makes the Creator happier than seeing His created beings _receive_ joy. You experience this same feeling when you derive happiness from seeing joy in your children or other loved ones. So it was that the Creator brought into existence beings that embodied pure receiving.

But the souls wanted to receive an additional gift. The souls desired the ability to share. Why? The Creator shares, and they wanted to emulate the Creator. In order to achieve this end, the souls of humanity—that means you and me—resisted the Light, the joy, and the answers that the Creator shared. We chose not to receive in order to have the opportunity to share.

In this moment, God withdrew His Light, leaving only a small, empty space that we call the universe. This would be the place, the playing field, where we could learn to share, where we as receiving entities could develop the power to impart happiness to another being.

God. You and me. Learning to share. That's all there is.

In Kabbalah, these components are called:

1. Sharing, also known as the Light
2. Receiving, also known as the Vessel
3. Free Will to Share or Receive, also known as Resistance

Together these three forces form the basis of all reality. They are all that really exists. And the simplicity of it all is really quite profound. Let's examine this idea further.

Kabbalah says the Light is not a physical entity but a form of energy, a force of consciousness. So was the original Soul. There was nothing physical in this original realm. There were only three forms of energy, three forms of consciousness: *sharing*, *receiving*, and *resistance*.

When our physical world came into existence, these three forces took on physical form.

At this point, Sharing, Receiving, and the force of Resistance became:

1. The proton (+)
2. The electron (-)
3. The neutron (0)

Only the names have been changed. A kabbalist calls the positive force the Light. A scientist calls it a proton. But they are talking about the same thing. A kabbalist calls the negative receiving force a Vessel. The scientist calls it an electron. Get the idea?

- The Creator is a sharing power, the positive charge (+).

- The Souls of humanity are the receiving power, the negative charge (-).

As you learned in high school, three forces—the proton, electron, and neutron—create an atom. You also learned that our entire world is made up of atoms. Alaskan sea bass and African zebras are made up atoms. So are you. So is your kitchen cutlery. The only reason a zebra looks different from a fork is the way its atoms are arranged. It's like Lego building blocks. You can build a car with Lego, or you can make a building with those very same blocks. Atoms can be arranged into the bodies of serial killers or peace activists. Everything is made up of atoms.

The electron, proton, and neutron that make up an atom are really forces of consciousness, or energy that creates the illusion of physicality. These three subatomic particles are merely *frozen* forms of these original three forces of consciousness. Consider H_2O. It can appear as a mist that cannot be held. Or you can freeze it, causing it to transform into ice that is physical and rock solid. The electron is merely the Vessel, the receiving force of consciousness in *frozen* form.

You see now the intimate connection between our own consciousness and every atom in our body. They are linked. They are one. This union of our atoms and our consciousness is one of the biggest secrets of Kabbalah, and understanding it is vital to understanding the power contained in the last three letters of this line.

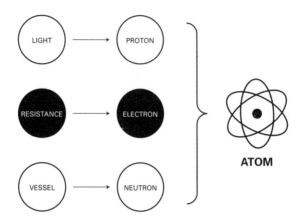

Kabbalistically, the entire world is made of the original Light, Vessel, and act of Resistance. Science says the same thing. Protons, electrons, and neutrons create an atom. The entire world is made up of atoms.

Sharing Prevents Cell Decay

Do you know why a zebra remains a zebra, specifically why the atoms that create a zebra do not suddenly rearrange themselves into a fork? Do you know why the atoms that make up the chair you're now sitting on do not suddenly fall apart and leave you on the floor? Did you ever stop and ask yourself that question?

Science gives us the answer. Atoms literally hold hands. That's right. Atoms hold the hands of neighboring atoms in order to bond together. The moment two atoms bond they form a molecule.

Do atoms actually have hands? No. The way atoms hold hands is by sharing electrons. Electrons are what bond atoms together, and remember that electrons are negatively charged. Remember, too, that electrons are receiving energy. So, atoms share electrons with other atoms and this is how they bond together to form molecules. These molecules, in turn, bond together to form everything in our physical world.

Here's the secret: Atoms mirror our consciousness. Atoms mirror our behavior. Why? Our consciousness and our atoms are the same thing. There is no difference between them. Our desire to receive is the electron. Our desire to share is the proton. Our free will to resist selfish receiving, to resist reactive behavior, is the neutron. When we share proactively, our atoms remain bonded together. Why? We are receivers by nature. When we share, we are using our receiving energy for the purpose of sharing. Atoms will now mirror this consciousness and continue to share electrons and thus bond with other atoms, forming the molecules that create the organs in our body. Each time we react, each time we behave with ego, each time we are selfish, a few hundred atoms let go of each other. This means a few more molecules cease to exist, and our body begins to deteriorate and age.

Kabbalah says aging and death occur because of reactive behavior. Each egocentric response brings a little death into our lives as atoms let go of each other and molecules die off. As cells die, the body dies. Line three, specifically *(YUD, KAF, SHIN)*, reverts our cells back to their original, healthy state, reversing the deterioration process. It changes the consciousness of the cell, specifically, the atoms that form the cell. Meditate on this sequence with an open and giving heart, and in your day-to-day activities exhibit this same kind of ego-less, proactive sharing in order to receive the maximum benefit from this incredible sequence.

What constitutes an act of selfless sharing? You'll know that you are sharing without ego when the act is extremely uncomfortable and difficult to carry out. When you give until it hurts (in the form of money or personal effort), your consciousness (every atom in your body) shifts into a sharing mode. In other words, your atoms keep sharing electrons and thus they remain bonded. When they do, your tissues and organs remain strong and healthy.

Never forget: when the body is used in a sharing manner, electrons are used in a sharing manner, which in turn renews the body.

This is the key to achieving immortality, and Heaven on Earth!

THE FOURTH LINE

THE FOURTH LINE – WEDNESDAY
BARKHEM TAHAREM RA<u>H</u>AMEY TSIDKATEKHA
TAMID GOMLEM.
BET, TET, REISH, TSADI, TAV, GIMEL

Giving up is easy to do. Throwing in the towel doesn't take much effort. But when we do, we fail to achieve our dreams and accomplish our goals. We compromise. We settle for less. *Quitting* is probably the most common of human attributes. It's no coincidence that the greatest achievers in human history all point to perseverance as the most important quality for achieving anything and everything. The letters in the fourth line of the 42-Letter Name of God point to the same thing.

How does the idea of perseverance apply to the path of human transformation and our quest to achieve ultimate fulfillment? Most if not all of us quit because we think we are not making any progress. We believe we are not making any headway. Obstacles obscure the goal line so we believe we cannot reach it. We experience constant setbacks. We feel an adrenaline rush in the beginning, but the moment we stumble and the rush wanes ever so slightly, we think that we need to quit the game entirely.

But obstacles, setbacks, and the appearance of no progress are, in fact, illusions meant to conceal the fact that we are actually achieving far more than we realize. We are blinded by the Adversary to the truth of our progress. We don't really understand what's happening when a setback occurs. We don't grasp the reality that underlies those moments when we fall.

We don't understand what obstacles really are.

Kabbalah explains it.

According to Kabbalah, there are ten dimensions that make up our reality. Two thousand years ago, this would have sounded like mystical mumbo-jumbo, but today it's called science. The study of fundamental physics and, more specifically, the field of string theory, point to the existence of ten space/time dimensions. That's right, both the modern-day scientist and ancient kabbalist agree that there are ten dimensions.

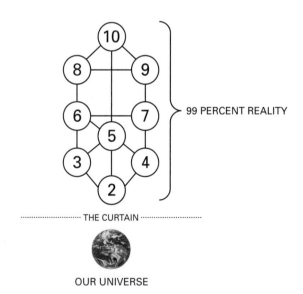

THE CURTAIN

OUR UNIVERSE

Each of these higher dimensions is part of the World of Answers, which is the source of all our Light. The higher you ascend into these spiritual worlds, the brighter the Light in your life. Each time we transform our nature, each time we rid ourselves of ego, we climb higher up the ladder.

THE LADDER

Two millennia ago, kabbalists told us that each one of these ten dimensions also has ten dimensions. In other words, there are ten levels of ten dimensions.

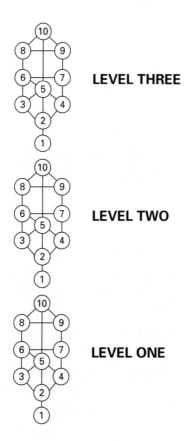

So, when you begin to climb the ladder of LEVEL ONE, you face obstacles. Impediments and challenges meet you every step of the way. When you finally reach dimension 10 on LEVEL ONE, you experience Light, blessings and joy. You feel as though you've accomplished great things. The path of Kabbalah appears wonderful and amazing. But guess what happens next? You now enter dimension 1 of LEVEL TWO. Suddenly, nasty new obstacles appear out of nowhere. A difficult challenge confronts you, and you begin to think that Kabbalah is not working for you any more. You feel as though are back on the bottom rung of the ladder. You feel like you fell.

Well, you are on the bottom rung. But this time you are starting at the beginning of LEVEL TWO—not LEVEL ONE! You have fallen up, not down. You are starting out in a whole new spiritual universe. To your five senses it feels as though you've taken ten steps backwards. In truth, you are higher than ever before. It's at this precise moment that the Adversary assails you with feelings of uncertainty, doubt, pessimism, failure, and his most dangerous weapon, discouragement. What do most people do? They quit.

Make no mistake: the higher you climb, the stronger the Adversary will become.

How do you battle his illusions? You need perseverance. Willpower. Resolve. Fortitude. And all the other synonyms in your thesaurus for the word *determination*.

Line four instills this power in you. It ignites your will to succeed. To never quit. To never give up. You receive the strength to keep on climbing. Most important, this line helps you to recognize that you are actually moving higher with each new step, with each new obstacle that you overcome. You realize that you are falling up, not down!

WINDOWS OF OPPORTUNITY

The last three letters of the fourth line have the same numerical value as the word "windows." The kabbalists tell us that this numerical connection reveals a wonderful secret. Windows let light in just as line four opens up windows into the World of Answers. This sequence becomes your skylight, allowing Light to fall upon you.

These windows also provide you with a superior view so that you can see the answers much more clearly. Just make sure you keep the windows clean. Wiping away your ego every chance you get is like taking window cleaner and a rag to the windowpane. Likewise, every time you react, every time you shout, every time you treat another human being with anything less than dignity, you smudge the window with dirt.

THE FIFTH LINE

THE FIFTH LINE – THURSDAY
HASIN KADOSH BEROV TUVEKHA NAHEL ADATEKHA.
HET, KOF, BET, TET, NUN, AYIN

This unique sequence in the 42-Letter Name of God is about clairvoyance, the ability to see far beyond the normal range of human
vision. But what does this really mean to you and me in our daily
lives? Without question, ancient kabbalists saw the future. They saw
the next day, the next month, the next decade, and even the next
millennium. But they were not prophets. They were not seers or psy-
chics as we commonly define such terms. Rather, the kabbalists
were masters of the law of cause and effect. We can use this same
law to our absolute advantage in our own lives.

Suppose a person, let's call him George, sees an egg for the very first
time in his life. George has no idea where this egg came from.
George has no idea what it is. One day the egg hatches. An adorable
chick emerges from the shattered eggshell. Though George has no
idea where the original egg came from, he now understands that a
baby chick can emerge from an egg. George is intrigued. He now
studies the chick for many years. He watches the chick grow into a
chicken. Then one day, the chicken lays an egg. The egg eventually
hatches. Wow. Now George understands the entire process. Next
time our friend George sees an egg he *also* sees the entire process
of *egg hatching, chick emerging, chick growing up into a chick-
en, and chicken laying new eggs*. George sees this at a glance,
just by viewing a single egg. From that single egg, a host of events
will unfold. Cause and effect.

Life works the same way. Just like the egg, our lives consist of a series of actions and subsequent reactions. Just as science tells us that for every action there is an equal reaction, so does Kabbalah. For every cause there is an effect. Everything is part of this process, and our lives reflect this natural law.

Kabbalists understand the process of cause and effect that under-lies everyday reality. If you plant an apple seed, you know that an apple tree will emerge with all the bark, branches, leaves, fruit, and new seeds for new apple trees. This is how kabbalists see the future.

NOTHING RANDOM

Every event in our world has a seed. If life appears chaotic, random, and disordered, it's only because we cannot perceive the process of cause and effect at work. In other words, we see the tree but not the seed.

This lack of perspective leads people to live under the illusion that things happen suddenly. They don't. They can't. Nothing occurs suddenly. An oak tree never just appears on your front lawn. A seed is always planted first.

If there is something in your life right now that you want to get rid of, you must first accept the principle that you—yes, you—planted its seed somewhere in your past. No matter how random the event appears to be, there are no accidents in Kabbalah. There is only order; cause and effect; action and reaction.

The Adversary would much rather have you point the finger of blame. Let's face it; it's easier to blame others for our misfortune. But by becoming accountable and taking responsibility for our actions, we are ensured far greater rewards than blame could ever provide. Do you know why? Taking responsibility is the ultimate act of seed-planting. When you accept responsibility for *everything*, you have just planted a seed that says: *I am in full control over my life and this world.* Do you know what happens next? A tree will grow in your life, with branches extending into every area of your existence, giving you absolute control over everything. When you plant a seed of control, you gain control. If you remain a victim, then your life will remain chaotic and random.

Now that you know life is about planting seeds, how do we continue to plant positive seeds instead of negative ones?

THE ART OF SEEING

Behavior is what makes one seed different from the next. Your reactive behavior plants negative seeds. Proactive behavior plants positive seeds. But knowing this is not enough. Why? When something chaotic in this world triggers a reaction within you, it's almost impossible not to react. The Adversary is constantly inciting reactions within you, which makes the planting of negative seeds seem almost inevitable sometimes.

The truth of the matter is that you can never summon the strength to stop a reaction simply because Kabbalah urges you not to react. That is not enough motivation. The only way you will stop reacting and put an end to unkind behavior is when you learn to recognize

cause and effect at work in the world. If you can foresee the repercussions of your actions, you will be motivated to stop your reactive
behavior. If you can see the future in the present moment, you will
change your egocentric behavior here and now. This is the only way.

But the Adversary blinds us. He tries to keep us from seeing the
future effects of our present actions. The Adversary only shows us
the immediate gratification that accompanies egocentric responses
to life.

Meditating on the letters in line five awakens clairvoyance. Here's
how: Line five increases your ability to foresee the consequences of
your actions. You become aware of the rewards and the repercussions triggered by your various modes of behavior. You come to
understand and perceive the value of resisting reactions and offer-
ing kindness. And you begin to do this not out of any high-minded
sense of morality, but because you see the payoff. Time no longer
deludes and confuses you. An understanding of cause and effect
drives your choices and your deeds.

In your daily life, the tremendous power that comes when you meditate on this line might reveal itself in ways like these:

- If you are maintaining a healthy lifestyle after a long battle
  with an addiction, the thought of picking up the habit again
  after a rough day will come complete with a vision of how
  empty and unhealthy you would feel after you get your fix.

- The impulse to drive in an unfriendly, aggressive manner will
  be immediately followed by the wisdom that behaving in

this way—although it might feel exhilarating for a second—can cause lasting pain and suffering.

- You will want to practice loyalty and honesty in your closest relationships, because you will instinctively recognize that every choice that involves manipulation and lying also involves heartache and profound spiritual trade-offs.

Line five bestows upon you all of the information you need to act wisely in every situation. In time, your every proactive decision becomes a positive seed planted. Soon your life becomes a sweet-scented orchard, lush with low-hanging fruit.

Kabbalists have a special name for making wise spiritual invest-ments (decisions) in the present, in order to bring about future abundance.

They call it Enlightened Greed.

As my father and teacher wrote about the Power of Enlightened Greed:

> If swindling and racketeering were the authentic way to receive lasting joy, the wise old kabbalists would have turned out to be the master swindlers and rack-eteers of all time. They would have given new mean-ing to the term "wiseguys".

> But the fact of the matter is, dishonesty and selfish-ness do not deliver the goods. Not because of morality,

but because of technology. Selfishness is just not part of the technology of Kabbalah or the universal laws of the natural world.

—Kabbalist Rav Berg

Kabbalists are a very greedy bunch; it's just that they are motivated by Enlightened Greed. In other words, they are motivated by the rewards that harmony brings. Decisions that are selfish and ego-based only deliver temporary pleasure. Lasting pain is always close behind, which makes it a pretty foolish bet. The payoff is lousy. It's bad business—plain and simple. So kabbalists engage in kindness, because it's the shrewdest long-term investment on the planet.

Why engage in practices that only make way for more emptiness, when you can have your cake and eat it, too?

Recognizing the Emptiness

The fifth line corresponds to the fifth millennium according to the biblical calendar, a time of great darkness and emptiness in the world. If we are born into darkness and we live in darkness all our lives, darkness is all we know. We settle for less. We accept darkness and pain as a way of life instead of striving for something better. This fifth line of text shows you the empty areas in your life. Once you identify the emptiness, you can strive to fill it with Light.

THE SIXTH LINE

THE SIXTH LINE – FRIDAY
YAHID GE'EH LE'AMEKHA PENEH ZOKHREY
KEDUSHATEKHA.
YUD, GIMEL, LAMED, PEI, ZAYIN, KOF

The sixth line relates directly to the sixth millennium according to the biblical calendar. What is the significance of the sixth millennium? Kabbalah tells us that the universe has been in existence for some 15 billion years, but human consciousness, the ability to transform and elevate our self and this world, has been in existence for 5,767 years at the writing of this book. According to Kabbalah, the six days of Creation and the seventh day of rest are a code for the seven millennia human life will spend on Earth. There will be six millennia of human transformation and the seventh millennium will see the dawn of world peace and immortality.

However, we do not have to wait the full term in order to usher in the age of world peace and the seventh millennium. As we've seen, there are two ways for human beings to rid the body of ego and transform themselves.

1. Embracing a spiritual path of personal transformation.
2. Suffering.

Both approaches work. The kabbalistic tools in this book allow us to transform spiritually so that the only pain we experience is the temporary pain that the ego feels. But suffering also cleanses the body of ego. It's up to us to choose which path we take.

The idea here is to ignite the promise of the seventh millennium now, to bring future reward into the present. How?

Line six helps to ignite the spreading of a unified, non-judgmental spirituality, Kabbalah, and specifically the dissemination of the *Zohar*, to the entire world. It accelerates that process. Why is it so important to share the *Zohar* and Kabbalah?

The answer to that is found in a very old story.

THE MOST FAMOUS STORY NEVER TOLD!

PART ONE: THE BEGINNING OF TIME

Once upon a time there was an infinite, wondrous world of Light, a radiant world where unending happiness was the one and only reality.

You and I were originally conceived and born into this extraordinary world. However, as we soaked up the Light in this exalted existence something occurred to us. Something was missing.

What was it?

It was a dream; a dream for something far greater, far more profound than an existence where we could only receive unlimited joy:

We dreamed of becoming the actual creators of this unimaginable fulfillment.

Our own Creator understood the innate longing that burned within us for He imbued us with his own Divine nature. And so, to help us realize our dream, the Creator withdrew a portion of His Light, forming a tiny space of darkness.

That microscopic space of darkness was our vast universe of pain and suffering. Here we would have the chance to find and reignite the Light and thus become the cause and reason for our living happily ever after.

PART TWO: THE SINAI STORY

Life in the physical world was far more challenging than we ever thought it would be. Not surprisingly, we quickly lost our way. Instead of finding the Light we hung up curtains by virtue of our own negative egocentric behavior, which only dimmed the Light further. As generations came and went the curtains became more numerous, and the darkness continued to expand.

Our suffering and our blindness caused the Creator unbearable pain, so He intervened. He gave the world a body of wisdom, a technology that would help us find our way, find each other, and thus find the Light.

It was called Kabbalah.

The giving of Kabbalah is what actually took place during the event known as Revelation on Mount Sinai some 3,400 years ago. When Moses ascended Sinai, the curtains were suddenly torn down and a splendorous Light shone throughout the world. Moses had used the wisdom of Kabbalah to unite the ten dimensions, to connect the World of Questions with the World of Answers. Darkness vanished. Death disappeared. Once again we tasted the Light that was our true origin.

This immortal Light and kabbalistic wisdom radiated from the two Tablets that God had given to Moses. The Tablets were not about Ten Commandments. They were a technology that brought the Light into our physical world through all ten dimensions.

Paradise was now at our fingertips.

But after centuries of negative existence, the souls of humanity had become accustomed to the pain, addicted to the darkness. Humanity was hooked on negative energy generated by the ego and we rejected the Light.

The only way to resolve the addiction was 1,600 years of rehab. It was a painful process of wars, persecution, and suffering, but a window of opportunity would soon appear on the horizon.

PART THREE: A SECOND REVELATION

Approximately 2,000 years ago, the two Tablets, which embodied the hidden Light and the wisdom of Kabbalah, reappeared in our world but in a radically different structure. The two Tablets rematerialized in the form of the two holy Temples in ancient Jerusalem.

The world had a second chance at paradise. The Light that had vanished from Sinai could shine once again if the world was ready to receive it.

A young kabbalist by the name of Joshua, the son of Joseph (also known as Jesus) saw the opportunity at hand. He tried to prepare humanity by sharing the essential teaching of Kabbalah, which was "Love Thy Neighbor." However, the only way to love thy neighbor is to first rid yourself of ego. It is only the ego that prevents you from loving another unconditionally.

The kabbalist called Joshua (Jesus) spoke about the arrival of the Kingdom of Heaven, which was code: "Kingdom" referred to our physical World of Questions. "Heaven" referred to the spiritual World of Answers. The "Kingdom of Heaven" was what would happen when the two worlds united! Joshua spoke about sharing such secrets with the world, about shouting them out from the rooftops. This daring young sage wanted to spread the secrets of the universe to all the world.

The great kabbalist known as Akiva and his comrades also recognized the opportunity. They too tried to ready the world by teaching Kabbalah. But the world was not ready. Intolerance and jealousy consumed the hearts of everyone, even Akiva's very own students. The results were devastating.

Both Temples were eventually set ablaze, reduced to ashes. Jerusalem was sacked. And all the kabbalists of that generation were assassinated by a corrupt religious establishment that harbored deep hatred for Kabbalah.

Rabbi Joshua (Jesus) was nailed to a wooden cross. Rabbi Akiva was skinned alive. The kabbalist known as Rabbi Ishmael had his face torn off. The kabbalist called Gamaliel was beheaded. However, later kabbalists told us that fault lay not with the Romans, but with those who were still unwilling to give up their egos and break their addiction to the physical world. According to the ancient sages, the deaths of these great kabbalists helped cleanse and purify darkness brought about by the intolerance of one human being to another.

With the Temples in ruins and the kabbalists slain, the wisdom of Kabbalah and the Light that it offered were in danger of being lost forever. So again the Creator intervened.

A second Revelation would take place.

The splendorous Light and the wisdom of Kabbalah was then revealed to the great Kabbalist Rav Shimon bar Yochai, who was the reincarnated soul of Moses.

Rav Shimon transformed this Light into a sacred set of books known as the Zohar. Make no mistake: these were no ordinary books, just as the Tablets on Sinai were not common slabs of stone and the Temples were not just holy places of worship. All the Light that was lost before was infused into every letter of this magical book. The Zohar was a dynamic, active reservoir of divine energy, a powerful force that embodied the promise of the perfection of the endless world.

However, because hatred in the human heart had caused the destruction of both Temples and the slaughter of the kabbalists, the Zohar had to be concealed from the world a little longer. These potent manuscripts pulsating with energy and Light were then buried, hidden beneath the city of Jerusalem inside the Ark of the Covenant for another 1,200 years.

PART FOUR: A FINAL REVELATION

When the 12th and 13th centuries arrived they represented our final chance at creating Heaven on Earth. The Knights Templar went to Jerusalem and began excavations in search of the lost wisdom of Kabbalah.

After a few years of digging, they eventually unearthed ancient kabbalistic manuscripts. The Templars could not decipher the strange Aramaic text so they brought the manuscripts to Toledo, Spain, a city where Kabbalah was flourishing. The manuscripts wound up in the hands of the great kabbalist Moses De Leon, who then published the manuscripts.

And so it came to pass that the wondrous books of the Zohar were revealed again.

The Zohar's sudden appearance caused a great stir. Rumors of a mysterious and amazing discovery spread like wildfire. Speculations about the Templar find were rampant. People spoke of it in the streets. Wild stories circulated from Spain to France. Everyone knew the Templars had discovered some ancient and powerful artifact, but only the kabbalists knew it was the Zohar.

When Moses De Leon tried to disseminate the Zohar publicly he triggered an uproar in the religious establishment. He was accused of fraud and forgery. He was called a charlatan, a snake-oil salesman and a despicable swindler. Nevertheless, the appearance of the Zohar literally transformed the world overnight, abruptly ending the 1,200 years known as the Dark Ages.

PART FIVE: THE RENAISSANCE

Like the mysterious monolith in the book 2001: A Space Odyssey, the Zohar elevated and transformed human consciousness by its mere presence and, in turn, guided the evolution of human civilization.

History bore proof. As a powerful book of secret teachings, Kabbalah's wisdom profoundly shaped the thinking of history's greatest thinkers: Pythagoras, Plato, Jesus, and Muhammad. As a book of life, it was the ultimate story of the human soul and its never-ending struggle between good and evil, light and darkness. The Zohar chronicled the greatest of all human endeavors—the effort to end the ultimate darkness—death!

The Zohar's words and teachings influenced the great poets, philosophers, inventors, and writers, from medieval times up through the Renaissance. Dante, Shakespeare, and da Vinci were all inspired by Kabbalah. The father of modern medicine, Hippocrates, said Kabbalah was the source of all scientific and spiritual wisdom. Isaac Newton and the great physicists of the Renaissance studied the Zohar, igniting the scientific revolution. In fact, Newton's discovery of the color spectrum is found inside the Zohar.

As a technology, the Zohar promised to connect the soul to the unlimited world of answers upon contact.

It was the power of Sinai, the power of the Light of Revelation, and nothing less!

Still, negative forces motivated by the Adversary returned in every generation and tried to keep this power from the people. Kabbalists continued to be persecuted and tormented. As long as the Zohar did not wind up in the hands of the people, the fires of human destruction would keep on burning. That was terrific news for those who profited from such fires, so they stopped at nothing in order to prevent the dissemination of the Zohar.

In the 18th and 19th centuries, some scholars and "the establishment" smeared the kabbalists and slandered the Zohar. It was called a dangerous poison and a book of lies and sorcery. Kabbalists who taught the teachings of the Zohar were ex-communicated and forced to flee their homeland.

But all that changed at the turn of the 20th century.

PART SIX: POWER OF THE PEOPLE

Despite an avalanche of protest and physical violence, the prolific Kabbalist Rav Yehuda Ashlag opened up the Zohar to the world by founding the Kabbalah Centre in Jerusalem in 1922.

In response, the religious establishment said the sacred Zohar must be studied only by the righteous, the pious, and the holy. It was a deceptively immoral argument. After all, if a person is suffering, or thirsty for the Light of the Creator, or in desperate need of a miracle, does he or she have to be pious and holy in order to call upon this great Light? Kabbalist Rav Ashlag didn't think so.

In the short time span of 75 years, the Kabbalah Centre branched out across the globe. The entire Zohar was translated into English for the first time in history and disseminated to all those who had a desire for it—to Jews, Christians, and Muslims, to all the peoples of the world alike.

Incredibly, more Zohars spread throughout the world in a short 75-year period than in all of previous human history. It was unprecedented.

Miraculous stories about the Zohar's Light and ability to banish darkness poured in every day. This was not surprising. As Rav Ashlag said and all the great sages knew, every Zohar in the hands of an individual literally restores a portion of the Light that has been lost since the thought of creation. And the essence of this Light was nothing less than miracles and wonders. The essence of this Light was the end of death and the arrival of immortality.

And so, the ultimate objective was profoundly simple: spread Zohars until such time that enough Light shines to forever eradicate pain, suffering, and death from the landscape of human existence. The original dream that burned in the depth of the human soul so long ago was now on the verge of being realized.

All that was needed was a critical mass.

It is now up to us, our generation, to write the final chapter in this, the oldest and greatest story the world has ever known.

We write this final chapter and bring the attainment of a critical mass closer to reality every time we meditate on the sixth line of text. In addition, this line encourages us to become teachers. When I use the word teach, I do not mean that we should preach to others. Preaching is not teaching. Teaching means being a living embodiment of the principles that you wish to impart. Teaching means you become a living example, a shining case in point of the techniques that can positively transform a human being and our world.

When people feel your Light and energy, when they witness the changes within you, they will want to know how you did it. They will want to know the source of your power. And that is when you can gently share the *Zohar*, the great Light that was lost on Sinai, and the answer to our search for truth. The sixth line imbues you with the desire and ability to share the gift of the *Zohar* with others, thereby facilitating the formation of Heaven on Earth.

THE SEVENTH LINE

THE SEVENTH LINE – SATURDAY
SHAV'ATENU KABEL USHMA TSA'AKATENU
YODE'A TA'ALUMOT.
SHIN, KOF, VAV, TSADI, YUD, TAV

While the sixth line draws us closer to Heaven on Earth, the seventh line refers directly to the perfect world, the seventh millennium. This is important because the seventh millennium is a time when the Adversary is long gone. He has been defeated and humanity has achieved a state of perfection. Self-centeredness and intolerance are eradicated from the landscape of civilization. A perfected world, overflowing with abundance and prosperity, will be the new reality. Fear, anxiety, envy, jealousy, worry, doubt, pain, and suffering will have been wiped off the face of the Earth. Even death will have met its final demise. The power of your true soul will be unleashed. Contentment and serenity beyond our current comprehension will become our status quo.

The power of the 42-Letter Name of God is that you can bring the seventh millennium into your life right now.

CONTROL

The seventh line empowers us with control over all aspects of the physical reality, including our own material body. For thousands of years, the Adversary controlled this world. He controlled our thoughts and he controlled our environment. During the last 5,767 years, humanity has struggled to gain the upper hand and wrest control from the Adversary. It's been difficult, as the blood-soaked landscape of human history so eloquently testifies.

Through the power of the seventh line, you can finally defeat your Adversary as you draw the infinite power and perfection of the future into your current situation.

The only prerequisite for achieving total perfection at this very moment is your willingness to let go of your ego and truly embrace everyone in your life, friend and foe, with unconditional love.

Of course, the Adversary will use every trick in the book to prevent you from doing just that. Thankfully, all the previous sequences in the 42-Letter Name of God give you the power to defeat the Adversary every time he attempts to keep you imprisoned inside the chaos and pain of the World of Questions.

This simple Prayer of the Kabbalist is not just the answer to all of our prayers. More importantly, it is the prayer to all of our answers.

CHAPTER SIX

RECITING THE 42-LETTER NAME OF GOD

THE BASIC RECITATION

אבג יתץ   ❶ חסד, יום ראשון Sunday, Chesed

אָנָּא בְּכֹחַ. גְּדוּלַת יְמִינֶךָ. תַּתִּיר צְרוּרָה:

tserura   tatir   yeminekha   gedulat   bekho'ah   ana

קרע שטן   ❷ גבורה, יום שני Monday, Gvurah

קַבֵּל רִנַּת. עַמְּךָ שַׂגְּבֵנוּ. טַהֲרֵנוּ נוֹרָא:

nora   taharenu   sagvenu   amekha   rinat   kabel

נגד יכש   ❸ תפארת, יום שלישי Tuesday, Tiferet

נָא גִבּוֹר. דּוֹרְשֵׁי יִחוּדְךָ. כְּבָבַת שָׁמְרֵם:

shomrem   kevavat   yihudekha   dorshey   gibor   na

בטר צתג   ❹ נצח, יום רביעי Wednesday, Netzach

בָּרְכֵם טַהֲרֵם. רַחֲמֵי צִדְקָתְךָ. תָּמִיד גָּמְלֵם:

gomlem   tamid   tsidkatekha   rahamey   taharem   barkhem

חקב טנע   ❺ הוד, יום חמישי Thursday, Hod

וְסִין קָדוֹשׁ. בְּרוֹב טוּבְךָ. נַהֵל עֲדָתֶךָ:

adatekha   nahel   tuvekha   berov   kadosh   hasin

יגל פזק   ❻ יסוד, יום שישי Friday, Yesod

יָחִיד גֵּאֶה. לְעַמְּךָ פְּנֵה. זוֹכְרֵי קְדֻשָּׁתֶךָ:

kedushatekha   zokhrey   peneh   le'amekha   ge'eh   yahid

שקו צית   ❼ מלכות, שבת Saturday, Malchut

שַׁוְעָתֵנוּ קַבֵּל. וּשְׁמַע צַעֲקָתֵנוּ. יוֹדֵעַ תַּעֲלוּמוֹת:

ta'alumot   yode'a   tsa'akatenu   ushma   kabel   shav'atenu

וָעֶד: לְעוֹלָם, מַלְכוּתוֹ כְּבוֹד שֵׁם בָּרוּךְ (בלחש)

va'ed   le'olam   malkhuto   kevod   shem   barukh   (silently)

← Scanning Direction

When reciting the 42-Letter Name of God, we group the words into three pairs by reciting two words in a row, pausing, reciting two more words, pausing, and then uttering the final two words.

The reason we recite two words at a time is that there is an angelic force that elevates our prayers into the World of Answers. Specifically, an angel has three pairs of wings, and three times two equals six. The number six has an encoded meaning. There are six dimensions we need to connect with in order to make contact with the World of Answers. An angelic force is like an elevator, lifting us into these six dimensions. When we recite each line by grouping the words into three pairs, we connect to three pairs of wings or the six dimensions that put us in contact with the World of Answers.

The idea of a pair, like the two wings of an angel, is significant for another reason. There are two parallel systems of energy that control every single day of the week, both spiritually and physically. These two systems of energy exist side by side. But only one system can be operating at any given time. The two systems are:

1. THE NEGATIVE ENERGY SYSTEM (-) THE ADVERSARY

2. THE POSITIVE ENERGY SYSTEM (+) THE LIGHT

By default, the negative energy system of the Adversary has complete control over the world and your life. This means from the moment you wake up you are under the direct influence of the Adversary. This is why you often find yourself in a state of low energy, tired, irritable, anxious, lethargic, wired, stressed, and out of control. But the Adversary is clever. He gives you brief bursts of energy to fool you into believing that you are not under his influence.

ANGELS OF THE DAY

The only way to rise above the Negative Energy System is to connect to the Positive Energy System of the Light. You do that by using a unique set of passwords. Kabbalah calls these passwords *The Angels of the Day*.

These angels or packets of energy are represented by sequences of letters that log you into the Positive Energy System so that you can download positive energy and blessings into your life. How do you activate each password? Simple. Just meditate on the sequence for the current day of the week for a few seconds. That's it. Eye contact (without pronunciation) is how we activate the sequences and log into this infinite reservoir of positive energy. Below are the password sequences for each day of the week.

As you meditate on or recite the 42-Letter Name of God, line by line, simply turn to the Angels of the Day page that correspond to the day and the line that you are praying and meditating on.

For instance, suppose it's a Tuesday. You recite line one (Sunday), line two (Monday), and line three (Tuesday). After reciting line three, turn to the Angels that correspond to Tuesday and make a visual connection. Then turn back to the 42-Letter Name and continue with your prayer, reciting line four, line five, line six, and line seven.

That's all there is to it. Very simple, but very powerful.

ANGELS OF THE DAY

יוֹם אָ יֱהֹוִה

SUNDAY

יַוַד הַיֵ וַיֵ הַיֵ יֵוַד הַיֵ וַאֵו הַיֵ
אַל עֹדִי יֹאוּלְדְפֹהֵהַיִייֵיֹאוּדֹהַהֵיֵ
אָנָּא בְּכֹחַ גְּדוּלַת יְמִינְךָ תַּתִּיר צְרוּרָה
אַבְגֵיתֶץ יֱהֵוֶה יֶהֵוֶה
סֶמַטֵוַרֵיֶה גֵזַרֵיאֵל וֵעַנָאֵל לְבֵוֵאֵל

ר"ת סֵגֹוּל

ANGELS OF THE DAY

יוֹם בְּ

MONDAY

יוֹד הֵי וָאוּ הֵי יוֹד הֵי וָאוּ הֵי וְאוּ הֵי יוֹד הֵי יוֹד הֵא וָאוּ הֵא

אל יהוה יאולדפההאאויאוודההאא

קְבֵל רַנַת עַמְךָ שַׂגְּבֵנוּ טַהֲרֵנוּ נוֹרָא

קַרְעְשְׂטָן ־יֵהֲוֹהָ יְהֹוָה

שְׁמְעִיאֵל בְּרְכִיאֵל אַהֲנִיאֵל

ר"ת שׂוֹא

ANGELS OF THE DAY

יוֹם גֹּ

TUESDAY

יוֹד הֵא וָאוֹ הֵא יוֹד הֵה וָו הֵה
אל אֲדֹנָי יָאולֹדֹפֹההֹהֹהֹיֹווֹדֹהֹהֹהֹה
נָא גִּבּוֹר דּוֹרשֵׁי יוֹזוֹדֹך כבבת שׂמרם
נַגְדִיכַשׁ יַהֲוֹה יהוֹה
וזיאל להֹדיאל מוזניאל

ר"ת וזלם

ANGELS OF THE DAY

יוֹם דֹ

WEDNESDAY

יוֹדֹ הֵא וֵאו הֵא יוֹדֹ הֵה וֵו הֵה
אל אדֹנֵי יִאוכֹלֹדֹפֹהֹהֹהֹהֹהֹוֹיוֹוֹדֹהֹהֹהֹה
בֹרכֹם טֹהֹרם רוֹזֹמִי צֹדֹקֹתֹך תֹמֹיֹדֹ גֹמֹלֹם
בַּטְרֶצְתֹגֹ יֵהֵוְהֹ יְהֹוֹהֹ
וֹזֹקֹיֹאל רֹהֹטֹיֹאל קֹדֹשֹׁיֹאל

ר"ת וֹזֹרקָ

ANGELS OF THE DAY

יוֹם הֵ

THURSDAY

יוּד הֵי וָאו הֵי יוּךְ הִי וְאו הִי וְאו הִי יוֹד הָא וָאו הָא

אל יהוה יאולדפההאאיאוודההאא

וֹסִין קָדִיעֹ בְּרוּב טוּבְךְ נַהֵל עֲדֹתֶךְ

וַזֵקְבְּטַנֹעֹ יֵהֹוָה יֵהֹוָה

שְׁמוּעֵאל רֶעֲמִיאֵל קְנִיאֵל

ר"ת שׁוֹרקֻ

(הֹקְבוֹץִ מַלְאָכָיו בֹּר"ת שׁוֹרקֻ)

Scanning Direction

ANGELS OF THE DAY

יום וו

FRIDAY

יוֹד הֵי וָוו הֵי יֵוד הֵי וָאו הֵי

אל שׁדי יאוכלדפההייאוודההיי

יוזיד גאה לעמך פנה זוכרי קָדוּשָׂתך

יְגְלְפָזָק יְהֶוָה יוהוווהו

שׂוּמוּשׂיּוּאוּלוּ רוּפוּאוּלוּ קוּדוּשׂוּיּוּאוּלוּ

ר"ת שׂרקָ

ANGELS OF THE DAY

לֵיל שַׁבָּת

FRIDAY
SHABBAT EVENING

יוֹד הֵי וָאו הֵי

שׁוֹעָתֵנוּ קַבֵּל וּשְׁמַע צַעֲקָתֵנוּ יוֹדֵעַ תַּעֲלוּמוֹת

שַׁקוּצִית יַהֲוָה יֶהֱוֶה יֵהֲוֶה יְהֲוֶה

שְׁמְעִיאֵל בְּרְכִיאֵל אֲהֲנִיאֵל

ר"ת שוֹא

סְמְטוֹרֵיָה גְּוֵרִיאֵל וְעֶנָאֵל לְבְוּאֵל

ר"ת סְגוֹל

צוּרִיאֵל רְזִיאֵל יוֹפִיאֵל

ר"ת צֵירִי

Shabbat has additional energy, so we have three separate angel connections.

← Scanning Direction

ANGELS OF THE DAY

יוֹם שׁוֹבֹת

SATURDAY
SHABBAT MORNING

יוֹד הֵי וֵיו וֵיו הֵי יֵוַד הֵי וֵיו וֵיו הֵי

שׁוֹעָתֵנוּ קָבֵל וּשְׁמַע צַעֲקָתֵנוּ יוֹדֵעַ תַעֲלוּמוֹת

עַקְוּצִית יֱהֹוָה יֱהֹוָה יֶהֶוֶה יְהוָה

שְׁמִעִיאֵל בִּרְכִיאֵל אֲהָנִיאֵל

ר"ת שׁוא

קַדְמִיאֵל מַלְכִּיאֵל צוּרִיאֵל

ר"ת קָמָץ

ANGELS OF THE DAY

מְנוּחַת שֹׁבת

SATURDAY
SHABBAT AFTERNOON

יוֹד הֵא וַאו הֵא יוֹד הֵא וָאו הֵא

שׁוֹעָתֵנוּ קַבֵּל וּשְׁמַע צַעֲקָתֵנוּ יוֹדֵעַ תַּעֲלוּמוֹת

שַׁקוֹצִית יֱהֹוֹה יֱהֹוֹה יֱהֹוֹה

שְׁמֹעִיאֵל בִּרְכִיאֵל אֲהֹנִיאֵל

ר"ת שוא

פַּדְאֵל תַּלְמִיאֵל (תוּמִיאֵל) וְֹסַדְיאֵל

ר"ת פַּתוֹ

←
Scanning Direction

LETTERS OF THE MONTH

Just as there are Angels (energy influences) that affect us on a daily basis, there are also monthly influences that impact our life. Below you will find sequences of Two Letters that give you control over each month. There is also a particular line of the 42-Letter Name that corresponds to each month, as shown in the chart below.

Scorpio	Aries	Pisces	Sagittarius	Aquarius	Capricorn
Mar-Hesvan	Nisan	Adar	Kislev	Shevat	Tevet
דֹג	דֹה	קֹג	סֹג	צֹב	עֹב
LINE THREE		LINE TWO		LINE ONE	

Cancer	Virgo	Gemini	Libra	Taurus	Leo
Tammuz	Elul	Sivan	Tishrey	Iyar	Av
וֹזֹת	רֹי	רֹו	פֹל	פֹו	כֹט
LINE SEVEN	LINE SIX		LINE FIVE		LINE FOUR

← Scanning Direction

THE CORRECTION OF THE SOUL

An ancient technology called *Tikkun Hanefesh*, or the Correction of the Soul, is to be used when you arrive at the line in the 42-Letter Name that corresponds to the particular month you are in. This great, healing meditation removes the blockages in your soul that have accumulated over time. Every time you have allowed your ego to rule over you, the energy centers of your body, much like chakras, have become congested with negative energy, causing illness and loss of vitality in the organs of your body. When we utilize the Correction of the Soul technology, we remove these blockages and heal the various ailments within the body that the blockages have caused. This is a very powerful healing tool.

The instructions for using this technology are as follows:

1. Meditate upon the Two Letters of the month (see chart). Visualize them above your head.

2. Glide your right hand over all the organs of your body while visually scanning the corresponding sequences as shown in the following illustration.

3. Remember that when you visualize the Light, see it as a brilliant beam removing all of your negative energy and traits, while simultaneously pouring love and kindness into those around you. Focusing your thoughts on how the Light can help others, will bring the most benefit to the world. That's the ultimate paradox. The more we think about others, the more the Light thinks about us.

TIKKUN HANEFESH

LEFT BRAIN מוח שמאל BINA בינה יֱהֱוֱהֱ **3**	SKULL גלגתא KETER כתר יָהָוָהָ **1**	RIGHT BRAIN מוח ימין HOKHMA חכמה יַהַוַהַ **2**
LEFT EYE עין שמאל **5** יהוה יהוה יהוה יהוה יהוה	NOSE חוטם יִ יִ הִ הִ וֹ וֹ הִ הִ	RIGHT EYE עין ימין **4** יהוה יהוה יהוה יהוה יהוה
LEFT EAR אזן שמאל **7** יוד הי ואו הה	**9** **8**	RIGHT EAR אזן ימין **6** יוד הי ואו הה
MOUTH פה **10** יוד הי ואו הי (אהיה) אחה"ע גיכ"ק דטלנ"ת זסשר"ץ בומ"ף			
LEFT ARM זרוע שמאל GEVURA גבורה יְהְוְהְ **12**	BODY גוף TIFERET תפארת יְהֹוּה **13**	RIGHT ARM זרוע ימין HESED חסד יֶהֶוֶהֶ **11**
LEFT LEG ירך שמאל HOD הוד יְהְוְהְ **15**	REPRODUCTIVE ORGANS YESOD יסוד יוּ הֹוּ וּוּ הֹוּ **16** <hr>FEET MALCHUT עטרה מלכות יהוה **17**	RIGHT LEG ירך ימין NETSAH נצח יְהְוְהְ **14**

Back of Neck/Base of the Head: I will arouse stem cells that will flow to every part of my body to regenerate all organs and body parts.

Right Brain: I will waken the will to share unconditionally with others and ignite thoughts to share without any hidden agenda.

Left Brain: I will pray for the power to use my desires for the purpose of sharing with others, instead of advancing my own self-interest.

Center Brain: I will ignite the strength to resist all selfish thoughts, all egocentric reactions, and instead to be thoughtful and proactive at all times.

Right Eye: I want to see only the good in others.

Left Eye: Blind me to the faults of others and allow me to only see and recognize my own faults.

Right Ear: I want to hear and listen to others and accept all criticisms. I want to only hear good things about other people, and to be completely open to opposing opinions and other ideas, no matter how much I disagree with them. I will hear the messages of the Light and listen intently to the desire of my soul.

Left Ear: I want to become deaf to the voice of my ego, and to hear only the whispers of my soul.

Right Nostril: Arouse mercy. Let me never judge others. I will give everyone the benefit of the doubt. Arouse sweet fragrances.

Left Nostril: Join the fragrances to smoke that ignites through my left nostril, creating a powerful incense that banishes the forces of death from my body.

Important Note: When you come to the nostrils, do one nostril at a time. Make sure you hold your right hand over your right nostril for a few seconds longer than your left nostril. What you are doing is arousing the forces of mercy, which corresponds to fragrance, through the right nostril. When you do your left nostril, you are now arousing the forces of smoke. When you unite fragrance with smoke, it becomes incense. The Zohar says this spiritual incense actually removes the forces of death from the body. Visualize the forces of fragrance being mixed with smoke as you glide your hand over your right and left nostrils. Now take this incense and visualize it as rays of Light that are removing death from your entire body as you continue on with the Correction of the Soul meditation.

Mouth: Banish death from the entire physical world. I will only speak well of others. I will not gossip or speak ill will of my friends or my enemies. The words I voice should always originate from my soul, not my ego.

Right Arm: All my physical actions should take into consideration the welfare of others and not just my selfish ego. Waken my will to share unconditionally.

Left Arm: Shut down my selfish desires and allow me to use my talents and ambitions to also serve the good of others.

Heart: Soften my heart. Open it. I want to feel the pain of others so that I can help alleviate their pain.

Liver and other internal organs: Remove the influences of my ego. Strengthen my soul. Remove all negative blockages from my arteries. Nourish all the nations of the world with Light.

Right Leg: I want to walk the path of the Light. Every step I take should take into consideration the welfare of others. Every step I take should take me one step closer to the Light.

Left Leg: Shut down my ego so that I never walk away from the Light into the darkness.

Reproductive Organs: Control all my selfish sexual desires so that I think of my partner ahead of myself. Unite the World of Questions with the World of Answers so Light flows throughout the world.

Feet: Remove death once and for all from the physical world. I want to walk on the path of transformation so that I may receive all the answers to all my questions, all the answers to my prayers.

THE ULTIMATE SECRET FOR ACTIVATING
THE 42 LETTER NAME

The power of the 42-Letter Name has been revealed to you. Its potential is tremendous, because it contains within it all of the power of Creation. Use this book as a tool every day, a reference for learning and practicing this transformative prayer. For your convenience, all of the steps for using the 42-Letter Name of God are listed here:

- Recite each line of the 42-Letter Name up to the line for the current day of the week.
- Turn to the Angels that correspond to that day and make a visual connection.
- Then turn back to the 42-Letter Name and continue reciting the lines.
- When you arrive at the line that corresponds to the month you are in, imagine the month's letters above your head in white light.
- After imagining the month's letters, perform the Tikkun Hanefesh/Correction of the Soul meditation.
- Finish reciting the 42-Letter Name of God.

Your understanding of the power behind the letters in the unique Name of God will grow as you practice the prayer regularly. When you use the Name, remember that its full power is only activated when you fulfill these two requirements:

1. Focus only on uprooting negative traits, instead of praying for yourself. These negative traits block the Light that is already there. When a trait is removed,

Light will suddenly appear in your life. Keep in mind that Light means getting what you need to truly fulfill you, and not necessarily what you want. What we want often fills us with pleasure momentarily, but leaves us feeling empty later. Getting what we need, however, is how we attain lasting fulfillment.

2. Pray for positive results for others only. Share your Light with others by praying for individuals who need certain assistance and blessings. They could be in need of financial help, physical recovery, or emotional healing. Send them the energy with deep conviction.

This is how the Prayer of the Kabbalist works. We focus on our negative traits; we send goodness and healing to everyone else. If you master this, you master the entire power of the 42-Letter Name of God, and you transform your life.

May you dwell in the World of Answers and may all of your prayers be answered, now and always.

MORE FROM NATIONAL BEST-SELLING AUTHOR YEHUDA BERG

The Power of Kabbalah

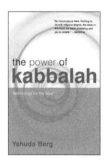

Imagine your life filled with unending joy, purpose, and contentment. Imagine your days infused with pure insight and energy. This is *The Power of Kabbalah*. It is the path from the momentary pleasure that most of us settle for, to the lasting fulfillment that is yours to claim. Your deepest desires are waiting to be realized. Find out how, in this basic introduction to the ancient wisdom of Kabbalah.

The 72 Names of God: Technology for the Soul™

The 72 Names of God are not "names" in any ordinary sense, but a state-of-the-art technology that deeply touches the human soul and is the key to ridding yourself of depression, stress, stagnation, anger, and many other emotional and physical problems. The Names represent a connection to the infinite spiritual current that flows through the universe. When you correctly bring these power sources together, you are able to gain control over your life and transform it for the better.

Angel Intelligence

Discover how billions of angels exist and shape the world, and how, through your thoughts and deeds, you have the power to create them, whether positive or negative. You'll learn their individual names and characteristics and their unique roles, as well as how to call on them for different purposes and use them as powerful spiritual tools for transformation. By becoming aware of the angel dynamics at work in the universe and by learning how to connect with these unseen energy forces, you will gain amazing insight and the ability to meet life's greatest challenges.

Rebooting: Defeating Depression with the Power Kabbalah

An estimated 18 million people in the United States suffer from depression—that's almost 10% of the population. So chances are good that you have, or someone you know has, been affected by it. Antidepressants, counseling, herbal remedies—all have been known to help treat the symptoms, but sometimes they fall short. If only you could click on the "Restart" button and get your internal software back on track. Now, in *Rebooting*, noted kabbalistic scholar and author Yehuda Berg shows how you can do just that by reconnecting with desire and light to emerge from this debilitating darkness.

The Living Kabbalah System™: Levels 1 & 2

Take Your Life to the Next Level™ with this step-by-step, 23-day system for transforming your life and achieving lasting fulfillment.

Created by Yehuda Berg and based on his belief that Kabbalah should be lived, not merely studied, this revolutionary interactive system incorporates the latest learning strategies, addressing all three learning styles:

- Auditory (recorded audio sessions)

- Visual (workbook with written concepts and graphics)

- Tactile (written exercises, self-assessments, and physical tools)

The sturdy carrying case makes the system easy and convenient to use, in the car, at the gym, on a plane, wherever and whenever you choose. Learn from today's great Kabbalah leaders in an intimate, one-on-one learning atmosphere. You get practical, actionable tools and exercises to integrate the wisdom of Kabbalah into your daily life. In just 23 days you can learn to live with greater intensity, be more successful in business and relationships, and achieve your dreams. Why wait? Take your life to the next level starting today.

MORE BOOKS THAT CAN HELP YOU BRING THE WISDOM OF KABBALAH INTO YOUR LIFE

Immortality
By Rav Berg

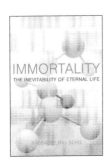

This book will totally change the way in which you perceive the world, if you simply approach its contents with an open mind and an open heart. Most people have it backwards, dreading and battling what they see as the inevitability of aging and death. But, according to the great Kabbalist Rav Berg and the ancient wisdom of Kabbalah, it is eternal life that is inevitable. With a radical shift in our cosmic awareness and the transformation of the collective consciousness that will follow, we can bring about the demise of the death force once and for all—in this "lifetime."

Wheels of a Soul
By Rav Berg

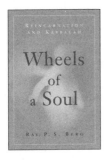

In *Wheels of a Soul*, Kabbalist Rav Berg explains why we must acknowledge and explore the lives we have already lived in order to understand the life we are living today. Make no mistake: You have been here before. Just as science is now beginning to recognize that time and space may be nothing but illusions, Rav Berg shows why death itself is the greatest illusion of all.

God Wears Lipstick: Kabbalah For Women
By Karen Berg

For thousands of years, women were banned from studying Kabbalah, the ancient source of wisdom that explains who we are and what our purpose is in this universe. Karen Berg changed that. She opened the doors of The Kabbalah Centre to all who would seek to learn.

In *God Wears Lipstick*, Karen Berg shares the wisdom of Kabbalah, especially as it affects you and your relationships. She reveals a woman's special place in the universe and why women have a spiritual advantage over men. She explains how to find your soulmate and your purpose in life, and empowers you to become a better human being.

The Secret: Unlocking the Source of Joy & Fulfillment
By Michael Berg

The Secret reveals the essence of life in its most concise and powerful form. Several years before the latest "Secret" phenomenon, Michael Berg shared the amazing truths of the world's oldest spiritual wisdom in this book. In it, he has pieced together an ancient puzzle to show that our common understanding of life's purpose is actually backwards, and that anything less than complete joy and fulfillment can be changed by correcting this misperception.

THE ZOHAR

Composed more than 2,000 years ago, *The Zohar* is a set of 23 books, a commentary on biblical and spiritual matters in the form of conversations among spiritual masters. But to describe *The Zohar* only in physical terms is greatly misleading. In truth, *The Zohar* is nothing less than a powerful tool for achieving the most important purposes of our lives. It was given to all humankind by the Creator to bring us protection, to connect us with the Creator's Light, and ultimately to fulfill our birthright of true spiritual transformation.

More than eighty years ago, when The Kabbalah Centre was founded, *The Zohar* had virtually disappeared from the world. Few people in the general population had ever heard of it. Whoever sought to read it—in any country, in any language, at any price—faced a long and futile search.

Today all this has changed. Through the work of The Kabbalah Centre and the editorial efforts of Michael Berg, *The Zohar* is now being brought to the world, not only in the original Aramaic language but also in English. The new English *Zohar* provides everything for connecting to this sacred text on all levels: the original Aramaic text for scanning; an English translation; and clear, concise commentary for study and learning.

THE KABBALAH CENTRE

The International Leader in the Education of Kabbalah

Since its founding, The Kabbalah Centre has had a single mission: to improve and transform people's lives by bringing the power and wisdom of Kabbalah to all who wish to partake of it.

Through the lifelong efforts of Kabbalists Rav and Karen Berg, and the great spiritual lineage of which they are a part, an astonishing 3.5 million people around the world have already been touched by the powerful teachings of Kabbalah. And each year, the numbers are growing!

• • • •

If you were inspired by this book in any way and would like to know how you can continue to enrich your life through the wisdom of Kabbalah, here is what you can do next:

Call 1-800-KABBALAH where trained instructors are available 18 hours a day. These dedicated people are willing to answer any and all questions about Kabbalah and help guide you along in your effort to learn more.

This work is dedicated to the memory of my parents
Itzkhak ben Avraham and Tzivia Bat Tovah.

May their souls be elevated to a higher level and
may their spirits reside among the Tzaddikim.